Southern Living. Cookbook Library

The Holiday Cookbook

Copyright© 1971 Oxmoor House, Inc.
All rights reserved.
Library of Congress Catalog Number: 76-45873
ISBN: 0-8487-0334-0

Cover: Apple Dumplings (page 152)
Left: Thanksgiving Roast Duckling (page 146)

contents

Ideas for your Christmas table begin on page 155.

preface

Holidays are a most important time to the people of the Southland. The calendar seems to roll quietly back while old and precious traditions emerge. As would be expected of people who treasure gracious hospitality and excellent cuisine, many of the South's holiday traditions center around the preparation and service of holiday foods.

Time-honored recipes are brought out as holidays approach. From thousands of southern kitchens come the appetite-teasing aromas of rich fruit cakes . . . exquisite dishes of meat and fowl . . . light-as-a-feather breads . . . and all the foods so important to holiday festivities.

Now you can share in the rich holiday tradition of the South. *Southern Living* readers have contributed the hundreds of tried-and-proven recipes that comprise this *Holiday Cookbook.* As you browse through the pages that follow, you'll discover typically southern holiday menus, recipes, table and room decorations. You'll find yourself in a marvelous new world, a world where food dishes have been developed and perfected for hundreds of years.

This book is your introduction to holiday foods and traditions destined to be as cherished by your family as they have been by generations of southern families. From our kitchens to yours, welcome to the wonderful world of holiday foods — southern style!

4

holiday menus

NEW YEAR'S EVE BUFFET

Hot Cranberry Punch p. 10
Anchovy Butter on Toast Rounds p. 12
Shrimp Dip Germaine p. 11
Cheese-Stuffed Pickles p. 12
Veal Roulet p. 16
Nicoise Mushrooms p. 18
Spinach Puffs p. 18
Orange-Fig Salad p. 14
Popovers p. 18
Almond Cheesecake p. 19
Elegant Eggnog Eclairs p. 20
Cafe Cappuccino p. 10

NEW YEAR'S DAY DINNER

Cheddar Onion Soup p. 21
Ham Wellingtons With Sauce p. 23
Good-Luck Black-Eyed Peas p. 25
Piquant Potatoes p. 25
Grapefruit-Celery Salad p. 21
Lucky Horseshoe Rolls p. 25
Kismet Cake p. 27

ABRAHAM LINCOLN'S BIRTHDAY

Hot Mint Tea p. 30
Circuit Rider's Stew p. 31
Thrifty Ribs p. 32
Whig's Corn Pudding p. 36

New Salem Yams With Pecans p. 36
Turnip Greens p. 36
Liberty Bread p. 37
Kentucky Prune Cake p. 38

ST. VALENTINE'S DAY LUNCHEON

Red Velvet Soup With Crouton Hearts p.43
Baked Snapper With Red Sauce p. 47
Green Onions With Anchovy Butter p. 48
Asparagus Salad With Beet Hearts p. 44
Beaten Biscuits With Lemon Butter p. 50
Fruit Flambe Loving Cup p. 50

GEORGE WASHINGTON'S BIRTHDAY

Tidewater Tea p. 54
Senators' Bean Soup p. 54
Little Hunting Creek Dove p. 58
Virginia Roast Pork With Cherry Glaze p.58
Cherry Tomatoes Vinaigrette p. 56
Southern Cornmeal Rolls p. 59
Mt. Vernon Steamed Pudding p. 60
Ratification Punch p. 54

EASTER FEAST

Almond Tea p. 67
Curried Egg Canape p. 67

Sea Kabobs (page 12)

new year

Winter is a bleak season in the South, a time when the rich earth and shining skies darken and turn the usually brilliant landscape colorless. In the midst of the dark winter's days come the twin bubbles of gaiety known as New Year's Eve and New Year's Day. Then joyous celebrating of the new year among friends and loved ones sends winter's gloom scurrying like a phantom.

What exciting traditions govern this holiday season! One, from tidewater Maryland, demands the serving of a dish called Hopping John, a flavorful mixture of peas, rice, and white meat. In times past, as this traditional dish arrived in the dining room, the children present would rise and hop completely around the table, returning to their seats in time to enjoy their share of the "good luck" food. So it is that on the New Year's dinner menu at the beginning of this book, Good-Luck Black-Eyed Peas are featured.

In the following pages, readers of *Southern Living* magazine share their most prized recipes, not only for peas, but for many other dishes certain to brighten up your New Year's holiday season — fondues and buffet dishes, meats, soups . . . elegant dinner and party foods. Every recipe is a family favorite that has won for its creator an enviable reputation as an excellent cook and hostess. These dishes can bring you the same kind of fame — try them and see.

Holiday Punch Bowl (below)

new year's eve

HOLIDAY PUNCH BOWL

1 46-oz. can cocktail
vegetable juice

1 tbsp. lemon juice
1/2 tsp. dried dill leaves

Combine all ingredients and chill. Pour into a punch bowl. 12 servings.

HOT CRANBERRY PUNCH

2 1/2 c. pineapple juice
2 c. cranberry juice
1 tbsp. whole cloves
1/2 tsp. whole allspice

1/2 c. (packed) brown sugar
1/4 tsp. salt
2 sticks cinnamon

Pour the juices into a 10-cup percolator and fill with water. Add the cloves, allspice, sugar and salt to percolator basket. Break the cinnamon into pieces and place in basket. Percolate through cycle. Additional sugar may be added, if desired. Serve hot. 12 servings.

Mrs. Doris Hartman, Neches, Texas

CAFE CAPPUCCINO

1/2 c. evaporated milk
2 tbsp. powdered sugar
1/4 tsp. vanilla

1/4 tsp. cinnamon
6 c. hot expresso type coffee
Grated chocolate (opt.)

Chill milk until half frozen. Add powdered sugar, vanilla and cinnamon; beat until thick and fluffy. Fill cups 1/3 full and fill with hot coffee. Top with grated chocolate. Hot percolator coffee may be used. Yield: 6 servings.

Mrs. T. E. O'Donovan, Fort Story, Virginia

CAFE CHOCOLATE

4 tsp. chocolate syrup or topping	1 tsp. vanilla
4 c. strong hot coffee	Whipped cream

Place 1 teaspoon chocolate in each coffee cup. Combine coffee and vanilla. Fill each cup and top with whipped cream.

Mrs. Larry Owens, Texarkana, Texas

APRICOT TEA

10 cloves	2 No. 2 cans apricot nectar
2 sticks cinnamon	1/4 c. lemon juice
1/2 c. sugar	3 c. tea

Tie the cloves and cinnamon in cheesecloth and place in a saucepan. Add the sugar and 1 cup water and stir until sugar is dissolved. Bring to a boil. Add the apricot nectar, lemon juice and tea and bring to a boil. Remove the cheesecloth bag and serve hot.

Mrs. Pat Jones, Enid, Oklahoma

SHRIMP DIP GERMAINE

1 lb. shrimp	1 lemon, sliced
1 bay leaf	2 lge. onions
1 tsp. mixed pickle spice	1/2 c. finely chopped celery
1/4 tsp. cayenne pepper	Mayonnaise
1 clove of garlic	

Place the shrimp in a saucepan and add enough boiling, salted water to cover. Add the bay leaf, pickle spice, cayenne pepper, garlic and lemon and cook for 10 minutes or until shells turn pink. Remove shrimp from water and cool. Peel and remove veins. Grind shrimp with onions and celery. Add enough mayonnaise to moisten. Serve with potato chips or snack crackers. 20 servings.

Mrs. A. V. Rachal, Alexandria, Louisiana

ANCHOVY BUTTER ON TOAST ROUNDS

10 to 12 anchovy fillets
1 c. clarified butter
1 tbsp. chopped parsley

1 tbsp. chopped chives
Crisp toast rounds

Rinse the anchovy fillets and chop fine. Place in a bowl. Add the butter, parsley and chives and mix well. Serve with toast.

Mrs. Joe Morris, Lumberton, North Carolina

CHEESE-STUFFED PICKLES

4 lge. dill pickles
1 3-oz. package cream cheese
Cream

Worcestershire sauce to taste
Crisp bacon bits to taste (opt.)

Cut off ends of pickles and remove centers with apple corer or potato peeler. Soften the cream cheese and add enough cream to moisten. Add the Worcestershire sauce and bacon bits and mix well. Stuff the pickles with cheese mixture and chill for 2 to 4 hours. Cut into 1/2-inch slices. Chopped pimento may be substituted for bacon bits.

Mrs. Juanita Goss, Avoca, Texas

COCKTAIL CHICKEN

1 fryer or stewing chicken
1 stalk celery, sliced
1 lge. onion, chopped
1 tsp. salt

Pepper to taste
1 14-oz. bottle barbecue
   sauce

Place the fryer in a saucepan and cover with water. Add the celery, onion, salt and pepper and bring to a boil. Reduce heat and cover. Simmer for 1 hour to 1 hour and 30 minutes or until chicken is tender. Cool and drain. Remove skin and discard. Remove chicken from bones and dice. Place in a saucepan and add the sauce. Simmer for 30 minutes. Serve hot in small buns. 50 cocktail servings.

Mrs. G. R. Moore, Jackson, Mississippi

SEA KABOBS

Scallops
Shrimp
Cherry tomatoes
Green pepper cubes

Seafood seasoning to taste
Melted butter
1 box Italian-style
   risotta rice

Place the scallops, shrimp, tomatoes and green pepper cubes on skewers and sprinkle with seafood seasoning. Grill over charcoal or broil in oven until done, basting frequently with butter. Prepare the rice according to package directions and place in a serving dish. Place the kabobs on rice and serve. Kabobs may be prepared a day ahead and refrigerated until ready to cook.

Photograph for this recipe on page 8.

DILLED SALMON MOUSSE

3 sprigs of parsley	2/3 c. finely chopped onion
2 ribs celery, cut in strips	2 tsp. Worcestershire sauce
1 carrot, quartered	2 tsp. salt
1 lge. onion, quartered	1/8 tsp. pepper
1 bay leaf	1 c. chopped dill pickle,
2 1/4 lb. fresh salmon	drained
1 c. sour cream	1 1/2 tbsp. unflavored
1 c. mayonnaise	gelatin

Place the parsley, celery, carrot, quartered onion, bay leaf and salmon in a large saucepan and add enough boiling water to cover. Simmer for about 15 minutes or until salmon flakes easily when tested with a fork. Remove salmon from stock and cool. Strain and reserve 1 cup stock. Discard vegetables. Skin the salmon, remove bones and flake. Blend the sour cream and mayonnaise in a large bowl. Add the chopped onion, Worcestershire sauce, salt, pepper, pickle and salmon and mix well. Soften the gelatin in 1/3 cup cold water. Bring reserved fish stock to a boil. Add the gelatin and stir until dissolved. Stir into salmon mixture and pour into an 8-cup ring mold. Chill until firm. Unmold onto a large plate and garnish center of ring with chicory and cherry tomatoes. Two 16-ounce cans plus one 7 3/4-ounce can salmon, drained, boned and flaked, plus 1 cup chicken broth may be substituted for fresh salmon and reserved stock. Reduce salt to 1 teaspoon. 8-12 servings.

Dilled Salmon Mousse (above)

ORANGE-FIG SALAD

1 No. 303 can figs	1 3-oz. package cream cheese
Juice of 1 lemon	2 tsp. Worcestershire sauce
Juice of 1 orange	1/4 c. chopped pecans
1 3-oz. package orange gelatin	

Drain the figs and reserve juice. Mix reserved juice, lemon juice and orange juice. Add enough water to make 1 3/4 cups liquid and pour into a saucepan. Bring to a boil. Add the gelatin and stir until dissolved. Cool. Chill until slightly thickened. Soften the cream cheese. Add Worcestershire sauce and pecans and mix well. Cover each fig with cream cheese mixture. Arrange figs in a mold so that each serving will contain a fig. Pour gelatin mixture over figs and chill until firm. Serve on salad greens.

Mrs. Alfred J. Gipson, Decherd, Tennessee

SHRIMP DIVINE

3 lb. fresh shrimp	Juice of 3 lemons
1 tbsp. vinegar	Pepper and salt to taste
2 onions, sliced	1 clove of garlic, minced
1 c. olive oil	

Place the shrimp in a saucepan and add the vinegar and enough water to cover. Bring to a boil and cook for 5 minutes. Drain the shrimp and cool. Peel and devein the shrimp. Place alternate layers of shrimp and onions in a shallow dish. Mix the olive oil, lemon juice, pepper, salt and garlic and pour over shrimp mixture. Refrigerate for at least 8 hours or overnight. Drain the shrimp and serve on lettuce. 6-8 servings.

Mrs. Douglas Ossenfort, Vero Beach, Florida

SALAD ROMANOFF

1/2 c. cooked asparagus	2 hard-cooked eggs, chopped
1/2 c. cooked string beans	1 tsp. fresh mixed herbs
1/2 c. cooked green peas	1/3 c. French dressing
4 radishes, sliced	1/4 c. mayonnaise
2 artichoke hearts, chopped	

Place all ingredients except the mayonnaise in a bowl and toss lightly. Refrigerate for at least 30 minutes. Stir in the mayonnaise just before serving.

Lucile Freese, Nashville, Tennessee

STUFFED PEPPER SALAD

Green peppers	Milk
Cream cheese	Lettuce

Cut a slice from top of each green pepper and remove seeds. Soften the cream cheese and add just enough milk to moisten. Pack in green peppers. Refrigerate until firm, then cut in 1/2-inch crosswise slices. Place 3 slices on lettuce leaf for each serving and garnish center of each slice with tiny sprig of parsley or a small strip of pimento.

Mrs. M. D. Lopez, Wichita Falls, Texas

ROCK LOBSTER CURRY AFRIKAANS

1 green apple	**1 c. milk**
1/4 c. butter or margarine	**1 tbsp. curry powder**
1 sm. onion, chopped	**3 8-oz. packages frozen**
1 clove of garlic, chopped	**South African rock**
1 ripe banana, thinly sliced	**lobster-tails**
1/4 c. flour	**Salt to taste**
1 c. light cream	**Cooked rice**

Peel, core and chop the apple. Melt the butter in a saucepan. Add the apple, onion, garlic and banana and cook until soft but not brown. Stir in the flour. Add the cream and milk gradually and cook, stirring constantly, until thickened. Stir in the curry powder. Drop lobster-tails into boiling, salted water and bring to a boil. Drain and drench with cold water. Cut away underside membrane with scissors and carefully pull out lobster in 1 piece. Reserve empty shells for serving condiments. Cut lobster into 1/2-inch crosswise slices and add to sauce. Season with salt and simmer for 5 minutes. Pour over rice. Serve with condiments such as carrot chutney, salted peanuts, sliced bananas, chopped cucumber, pineapple chunks, coconut and avocado slices. 6 servings.

Rock Lobster Curry Afrikaans (above)

VEAL ROULET

1 6-lb. leg of veal	2 sm. garlic cloves, thinly sliced
2 tsp. seasoned salt	3 tbsp. flour
1 tsp. pepper	1/4 c. shortening
1/2 tsp. thyme	1/2 c. minced onion
1 c. white wine	1 c. chopped celery
2 c. canned tomatoes	1 bay leaf
1 onion, thinly sliced	1 c. beef bouillon

Place the veal in a shallow pan and sprinkle with seasoned salt, pepper and thyme. Combine 1/4 cup wine, 1 cup tomatoes and the sliced onion and pour over veal. Refrigerate for 2 hours, turning veal frequently. Remove veal and drain. Cut small slits in veal and insert garlic slices. Dust with flour. Heat the shortening in a Dutch oven. Add the minced onion and celery and cook until lightly browned. Add the veal and brown lightly. Place rack under veal. Add bay leaf, bouillon and remaining wine and tomatoes and cover. Roast in 325-degree oven for 2 hours and 30 minutes. Remove cover and roast for 30 minutes longer or until browned. Serve veal with sauce and garnish with cinnamon apples.

Mrs. Margaret Hamilton, Prattville, Alabama

BEEF CURRY

1/4 c. flour	2 c. sliced onions
1 1/8 tsp. salt	1/2 clove of garlic, minced
1/8 tsp. pepper	1 tsp. curry powder
1 lb. round steak	1 beef bouillon cube
1/4 c. salad oil	1 c. boiling water

Hoska (page 17)

Combine the flour, salt and pepper. Cut the steak in small cubes and coat steak with the flour mixture. Brown in the oil in a skillet. Add the onions and garlic and cook until lightly browned. Sprinkle with curry powder. Add the bouillon cube and water and cover. Simmer for 1 hour and 15 minutes or until beef is tender, adding water, if needed. Serve over rice or mashed potatoes. 4 servings.

Betty D. Nicholson, Brevard, North Carolina

BEEF BURGUNDY

2 lb. beef chuck	1 c. Burgundy
2 tbsp. salad oil	1/4 c. water
1 med. onion, thinly sliced	1 beef bouillon cube
1 bay leaf	1/2 tsp. salt
1/2 tsp. dried thyme	1/4 tsp. pepper

Cut the beef in 2-inch cubes and brown in salad oil in a skillet. Place in a casserole. Combine remaining ingredients in a saucepan and bring to a boil, stirring frequently. Pour over the beef and cover. Bake at 325 degrees for 3 hours, adding water, if necessary. 4 servings.

Mrs. Raymond Boylan, Montgomery, Alabama

HOSKA

5 1/4 to 6 1/4 c. unsifted flour	1/4 c. chopped citron
3/4 c. sugar	1/4 c. seedless raisins
1/2 tsp. salt	1/4 c. chopped blanched almonds
2 pkg. dry yeast	Melted margarine
3/4 c. milk	1/4 c. whole blanched almonds
1/2 c. margarine	
3 eggs, at room temperature	

Mix 1 1/2 cups flour, sugar, salt and yeast in a large bowl. Combine the milk, 1/2 cup water and margarine in a saucepan and cook over low heat until liquids are warm. Margarine does not need to melt. Add to sugar mixture gradually and beat for 2 minutes with electric mixer at medium speed, scraping bowl occasionally. Add 2 eggs and 1 cup flour and beat at high speed for 2 minutes, scraping bowl occasionally. Stir in enough remaining flour to make a soft dough. Turn out onto lightly floured board and knead for 8 to 10 minutes or until smooth and elastic. Place in a greased bowl and turn to grease top. Cover and let rise in warm place, free from draft, for about 50 minutes or until doubled in bulk. Punch down and turn out onto lightly floured board. Knead in the citron, raisins and chopped almonds until well distributed. Divide into 4 equal pieces and set 2 pieces aside. Divide 1 piece into 3 equal strips 14 inches long. Place strips on a large greased baking sheet and braid. Brush with melted margarine. Divide 2/3 of the second piece into 3 equal strips 12 inches long and braid. Place on top of first braid and brush with melted margarine. Divide remaining piece of dough into 3 strips 10 inches long and braid. Place on top of second braid and brush with melted margarine. Repeat with remaining dough. Cover and let rise in a warm place, free from draft, for about 1 hour or until doubled in bulk. Beat remaining egg with 1 tablespoon water until well blended and brush over loaves. Decorate with whole almonds. Bake in 375-degree oven for 35 minutes or until done. Remove from baking sheets and cool on wire racks. 2 loaves.

HERBED BREAD

1 pkg. dry yeast	1/2 tsp. nutmeg
1 1/4 c. warm water	1/2 tsp. crumbled sage
2 tbsp. soft shortening	3 c. sifted flour
2 tsp. salt	Melted butter
1 tsp. caraway seed	

Dissolve the yeast in water in a bowl and add shortening and salt. Mix the caraway seed, nutmeg, sage and 1 1/2 cups flour and add to yeast mixture. Beat with mixer for 2 minutes or 300 strokes by hand. Add remaining flour and mix with spoon until smooth. Cover and let rise in warm place for 30 minutes. Stir down, beating 25 strokes. Spread in greased 9 x 5 x 3-inch loaf pan and let rise for 40 minutes. Bake at 350 degrees for 45 minutes or until bread tests done. Brush top with melted butter.

Mrs. Joseph J. Shippen, Atlanta, Georgia

POPOVERS

2 eggs	1/2 tsp. salt
1 c. milk	1 tbsp. melted shortening
1 c. sifted all-purpose flour	

Place the eggs in a bowl and add milk, flour and salt. Beat with electric or rotary beater for 1 minute and 30 seconds. Add the shortening and beat for 30 seconds longer. Do not overbeat. Fill 6 to 8 well-greased muffin cups 1/2 full. Bake at 475 degrees for 15 minutes. Reduce temperature to 350 degrees and bake for 25 to 30 minutes longer or until browned. Prick each popover with a fork to let steam escape and bake for 5 minutes longer. Serve hot.

Mrs. Roy Dawson, Lexington, Kentucky

NICOISE MUSHROOMS

1 1/2 lb. fresh mushrooms	1 tsp. salt
1/2 c. melted butter	1/4 tsp. pepper
1 tbsp. chopped marjoram	1 c. chicken bouillon
1 tsp. minced chives	1/4 c. Chablis

Preheat oven to 350 degrees. Wash the mushrooms and place in a greased casserole. Combine the butter, marjoram, chives, salt and pepper. Add the bouillon and Chablis and stir well. Pour over mushrooms and cover. Bake for 20 minutes. Canned mushrooms, drained, may be substituted for fresh mushrooms.

Mrs. Otis Goodrich, Cumberland, Maryland

SPINACH PUFFS

2 c. cooked spinach	1/2 to 1 tsp. salt
2 tbsp. melted butter	1/4 tsp. pepper

2 eggs
Bread crumbs
2 tbsp. grated onion
2 tbsp. grated cheese

1/8 tsp. allspice
1/4 tsp. oregano
1/4 c. water

Combine the spinach, butter, salt, pepper, 1 egg, 1 cup bread crumbs, onion, cheese and spices and refrigerate for 10 minutes. Shape into balls. Beat remaining egg and stir in the water. Roll the spinach balls in bread crumbs, then in egg mixture. Roll in crumbs again. Fry in deep fat at 375 degrees until brown and drain on absorbent paper. 6 servings.

Mrs. Reva Bishop, Vine Grove, Kentucky

DATE-ORANGE CAKE

1 c. shortening
2 c. sugar
4 eggs
1 1/2 c. buttermilk
1 tsp. soda

1 tsp. salt
4 c. sifted flour
1 c. chopped dates
1 tsp. grated orange rind

Cream the shortening, sugar and eggs in a bowl. Mix the buttermilk and soda. Sift the salt and flour together and add to creamed mixture alternately with dates, orange rind and buttermilk mixture. Place in a large, greased tube pan. Bake at 350 degrees for 1 hour and 15 minutes to 1 hour and 30 minutes.

Sauce

2 c. sugar
1 c. orange juice

Grated rind of 1 orange

Combine all ingredients in a saucepan and bring to a boil. Pour over hot cake and let set until cold.

Mrs. Dan Boggs, Richmond, Virginia

ALMOND CHEESECAKE

1 1/2 lb. ricotta cheese
2 tbsp. honey

1 tbsp. cream sherry
1/2 c. ground almonds

Combine the cheese, honey and sherry in a bowl and beat until well blended. Grease a 1-quart mold lightly and dust with small amount of ground almonds. Add remaining almonds to cheese mixture and mix well. Press into the mold and cover. Chill for 24 hours. Dip into hot water to unmold and garnish with seeded grapes or fresh berries. Catawba wine may be substituted for sherry. 6-8 servings.

Mrs. Robert B. Wood, Norfolk, Virginia

ELEGANT EGGNOG ECLAIRS

1/2 c. water	2 c. prepared eggnog
1/4 c. butter	1 tbsp. rum (opt.)
1/2 c. sifted flour	Whipped cream
1/8 tsp. salt	Butterscotch or chocolate
2 eggs	sauce
2 1/2 tbsp. cornstarch	

Place the water and butter in a saucepan and bring to a boil, stirring until butter is melted. Add the flour and salt all at once and cook, stirring constantly, until mixture forms a ball and leaves side of saucepan. Remove from heat and add the eggs, one at a time, beating well after each addition. Beat for about 5 minutes or until mixture has a silky sheen. Place dough, 1 tablespoon at a time, on a greased baking sheet and spread into oblong shape until about 4 inches long. Bake in 400-degree oven 30 minutes. Cool. Slice off tops with a sharp knife and remove soft dough from inside eclair shells. Place the cornstarch in a small saucepan and stir in eggnog gradually. Cook over medium heat, stirring constantly, until mixture thickens and boils. Remove from heat and cool, stirring occasionally. Stir in the rum and refrigerate until chilled. Fill eclair shells with eggnog mixture. Top with whipped cream and drizzle with sauce.

Mrs. Paul R. Beauchamp, New Orleans, Louisiana

SYLLABUB

1 c. fresh peaches, sliced	1 c. whipping cream
1 tbsp. lemon juice	1 egg white
5/8 c. powdered sugar	2 tbsp. sherry

Combine the peaches, lemon juice and 2 tablespoons sugar in a bowl and set aside. Beat the whipping cream with 1/4 cup sugar until stiff. Beat the egg white until stiff, adding remaining sugar gradually. Fold in the whipped cream. Fold in the sherry and pour over peach mixture. Pineapple or bananas may be substituted for peaches, if desired. 4 servings.

Nell W. Pantell, Jefferson, Georgia

new year's day

NEW YEAR'S DAY BONHEUR PEA SOUP

3/4 c. black-eyed peas	2 slices bacon
6 c. water	1 sm. onion, chopped
3/4 tsp. salt	1 tbsp. (heaping) flour
1/8 tsp. pepper	4 tbsp. bacon drippings
1/2 tsp. garlic salt	

Combine first 7 ingredients in a 2-quart saucepan and bring to a boil. Reduce heat and simmer until peas are tender, adding water, if needed. Cook the flour in bacon drippings in a small saucepan until lightly browned, then stir in 1 cup liquid from soup. Stir back into the soup and cook for 5 minutes longer.

Mrs. Joe F. Dornak, Louise, Texas

CHEDDAR-ONION SOUP

1 1/2 c. sliced onions	1/4 c. grated sharp Cheddar
3 tbsp. butter	cheese
1 1/2 qt. beef bouillon	6 slices French bread, toasted
1/4 tsp. salt	Grated Parmesan cheese
1/4 tsp. ground pepper	

Saute the onions in butter in a saucepan until tender. Add bouillon, salt and pepper and simmer for 30 minutes. Sprinkle Cheddar cheese over French bread and place bread on a cookie sheet. Broil until cheese is melted. Pour the soup into soup bowls and float toast on soup. Sprinkle with Parmesan cheese.

Katherine McAllister, Ferriday, Louisiana

CROESUS' NEW YEAR'S SALAD

3 c. mayonnaise	2 c. sliced celery
1 tsp. curry powder	2 to 3 c. slivered toasted
2 tbsp. soy sauce	almonds
2 qt. chopped cooked turkey	1 lge. can pineapple chunks,
1 lge. can water chestnuts,	drained
sliced	2 cans mandarin oranges,
2 lb. seedless grapes	drained

Mix the mayonnaise with curry powder and soy sauce. Add remaining ingredients and mix. Chill for several hours. Serve on lettuce leaves and sprinkle with additional almonds. Chicken may be substituted for turkey. 12 servings.

Mrs. Leland McInnis, Clemson, South Carolina

GRAPEFRUIT-CELERY SALAD

1 3-oz. package lime gelatin	3/4 c. drained grapefruit
1 tbsp. vinegar	sections
1/2 c. mayonnaise	3/4 c. diced celery
1/4 tsp. salt	1 tbsp. diced onion
Dash of pepper	

Dissolve the gelatin in 1 cup hot water in a bowl. Add 1/2 cup cold water, vinegar, mayonnaise, salt and pepper and stir until blended. Chill until partially congealed, then whip until fluffy. Fold in grapefruit, celery and onion and pour into a mold. Refrigerate until firm. Cut in squares and serve on lettuce. 6 servings.

Mrs. Ella G. Carter, Bradenton, Florida

Walnut Salad Athena (below)

WALNUT SALAD ATHENA

2 tbsp. butter
1/2 tsp. crumbled dried
  rosemary
1 c. walnut halves or lge.
  pieces
3/4 c. French dressing
2 c. cooked cleaned lge.
  shrimp
1 tbsp. finely chopped parsley
2 tbsp. finely chopped chives
Crisp salad greens

6 whole or sliced radishes
6 whole or sliced pitted ripe
  olives
6 whole or sliced stuffed
  green olives
1/2 c. small pickled onions
3 med. firm ripe tomatoes,
  cut in wedges
3/4 c. crumbled feta or cubed
  Jack cheese

Melt the butter with rosemary in a heavy skillet. Add the walnuts and cook over low heat, stirring occasionally, for 10 minutes or until walnuts are lightly toasted. Remove from heat and cool. Pour the French dressing over the shrimp in a bowl. Add the parsley and chives and mix gently. Cover and marinate in refrigerator for 1 hour or longer, stirring frequently. Line a chilled serving dish with salad greens. Add walnuts and remaining ingredients to shrimp and mix well. Arrange on greens. 6 servings.

SPANISH ONION SALAD

Spanish onions
Oil-vinegar dressing

Anchovies
Salt and pepper to taste

Cut the onions in very thin slices and place in a bowl. Cover with oil-vinegar dressing and refrigerate for 30 minutes. Add the anchovies and toss. Drain. Add the salt and pepper and mix well.

Mrs. H. W. Brooker, Maitland, Florida

GREEN SALAD BOWL

Salad greens	6 slices bacon
2 hard-boiled eggs, sliced	1 tbsp. flour
2 tbsp. chopped parsley	3/4 c. water
3 boiled potatoes, sliced	1/2 c. vinegar
Sliced cucumbers to taste (opt.)	1 tbsp. sugar
Sliced tomatoes to taste (opt.)	2 eggs, beaten

Line a salad bowl with greens. Arrange the eggs around edge of bowl and sprinkle with the parsley. Place the potatoes in the center and add the cucumbers and tomatoes. Fry the bacon in a skillet until crisp. Remove from skillet and drain. Crumble and sprinkle on the tomatoes. Mix flour with the bacon grease and add water, vinegar and sugar. Cook until slightly thickened, then cook for 5 minutes. Add the eggs gradually. Return to heat and bring to a boil. Pour over the salad mixture.

Mrs. Maude Pfaff Dunn, Winston-Salem, North Carolina

BEEF RING

2 lb. ground beef	1 med. onion, minced
1 c. packaged stuffing mix	2 tsp. salt
1/4 c. milk	1 1/4 tsp. hot sauce
2 eggs	

Combine all ingredients and mix well. Pack into a greased 9-inch ring mold. Bake at 350 degrees for 45 to 50 minutes. Remove from the mold and place on a platter. Center may be filled with mashed potatoes. 6-8 servings.

Berdie Fox, Dawson Springs, Kentucky

HAM WELLINGTONS WITH SAUCE

3 c. ground smoked ham	1/2 tsp. poultry seasoning
1 sm. onion, minced	2 pkg. pie crust mix
3 eggs	1 16-oz. can whole cranberry
6 slices bread, crumbled	sauce
1 c. cranberry juice cocktail	1/4 c. horseradish

Combine the ham, onion, 2 eggs, bread, cranberry juice cocktail and poultry seasoning and shape into 8 round patties. Prepare the pie crust mix according to package directions and roll out 1/2 inch thick on a floured board. Cut into 8 round pieces 2 inches larger than the patties. Wrap the pastry around the patties and pinch edges together securely. Place, smooth side up, on a large greased cookie sheet. Beat the remaining egg well and brush over pastry. Cut the remaining pastry into bell and scythe shapes and place on top to decorate each pastry round. Bake at 425 degrees for 25 to 30 minutes or until brown. Combine the cranberry sauce and horseradish in a saucepan and heat until bubbly. Spoon over the Ham Wellingtons. 8 servings.

Mary R. Barnum, San Marcus, California

Holiday Buffet Ham (below)

HOLIDAY BUFFET HAM

1 12 to 14-lb. fully cooked ham	Yellow food coloring (opt.)
4 env. unflavored gelatin	Pimentos
1 c. dill pickle liquid	Small sweet gherkins
2 c. mayonnaise	Scallion tops
6 tsp. prepared mustard	Watercress
	1/4 c. chopped dill pickles

Place the ham in a shallow roasting pan. Bake in a 325-degree oven for 15 minutes per pound or until meat thermometer registers 130 degrees. Cool and trim rind and fat evenly. Chill ham thoroughly, then place on rack in a clean, shallow roasting pan. Sprinkle 3 envelopes gelatin over 1 3/4 cups water in a saucepan and stir over low heat until gelatin is dissolved. Blend the pickle liquid with 1 cup mayonnaise and 2 teaspoons mustard in a medium bowl and stir in gelatin. Add several drops of food coloring. Place bowl in a larger bowl with ice and stir until mixture thickens to consistency of unbeaten egg white. Pour over the ham slowly. Leave the ham on rack and place on waxed paper in refrigerator. Chill until glaze is set. Pour glaze that has fallen into roasting pan back into bowl. Reheat glaze, if necessary, and chill again to thickened consistency. Repeat glazing and chilling ham until all glaze is used. Soften remaining gelatin in 1 cup water in a saucepan and stir over low heat until dissolved. Cool thoroughly. Arrange flower decoration on ham, using slices of pimentos and gherkins for flowers and scallion tops for leaves and stems. Dip each piece of decoration in clear glaze before applying to ham and use toothpicks, when necessary, to keep decoration in place. Cut out different shapes of pimentos with sharp scissors or knife and halve gherkins to arrange in a border around ham, dipping in clear glaze before placing on ham. Chill to set decoration. Pour remaining clear glaze over ham and chill. Garnish ham with watercress. Mix remaining mayonnaise with dill pickles and remaining mustard and serve with ham. 24 servings.

GOOD LUCK BLACK-EYED PEAS

2 No. 2 cans black-eyed peas	1/4 c. finely chopped onion
1/3 c. peanut oil	1/2 tsp. salt
1/3 c. wine vinegar	Cracked pepper to taste
1 clove of garlic	

Drain the peas and place in a bowl. Add remaining ingredients and mix well. Place in refrigerator for 24 hours. Remove the garlic and refrigerate for 2 days before serving. 6-8 servings.

Mrs. Rachel Pearce, Fort Worth, Texas

PIQUANT POTATOES

2 tbsp. chopped onion	2 c. cooked cubed potatoes
2 tbsp. diced green pepper	2 tbsp. chopped pimento
3 tbsp. butter or margarine	Salt and pepper to taste
1/2 c. chopped cooked ham	

Saute the onion and green pepper in the butter in a saucepan until tender. Add remaining ingredients and heat through. 4-6 servings.

Mrs. Mary Light, Kingsville, Texas

LUCKY HORSESHOE ROLLS

1 c. shortening	1 tsp. salt
1 c. hot milk	3 eggs, separated
1 pkg. yeast	1 c. raisins
1/2 c. warm water	1 c. chopped pecans
4 c. flour, sifted	1 can flaked coconut
Sugar	

Melt the shortening in the milk and cool to lukewarm. Dissolve the yeast in warm water. Place the flour in a bowl. Add 3 tablespoons sugar, salt, egg yolks, shortening mixture and yeast and mix well. Let rise until doubled in bulk. Chill for 2 hours. Divide dough into 3 parts and roll out each part into a circle. Beat the egg whites until stiff, adding 1 cup sugar gradually. Spread evenly over dough and sprinkle with raisins, pecans and coconut. Cut each circle into 8 wedges. Roll each wedge from wide end to point and place on a greased baking sheet, point side down. Shape each roll into a horseshoe and let rise for 30 minutes. Bake at 350 degrees for 30 minutes or until lightly browned. Ice with powdered sugar icing and sprinkle with additional pecans, coconut and raisins, if desired. 24 servings.

Mrs. J. S. Hood, Kershaw, South Carolina

Festive Peach Balls (below)

FESTIVE PEACH BALLS

2 1-lb. 13-oz. cans cling
   peach halves
2 3-oz. packages cream
   cheese
2 tsp. honey

5 tsp. Cointreau or orange
   juice
Dash of salt
1/2 c. mixed candied fruits

Drain the peaches and reserve 1 1/2 cups syrup. Soften the cream cheese in a bowl. Add the honey, 2 teaspoons Cointreau and salt and mix well. Spoon into cut side of 6 peach halves and top each with a peach half to make balls. Chill. Cook reserved syrup in a saucepan until reduced to 3/4 cup. Add remaining Cointreau and candied fruits and boil for 2 minutes. Cool. Place the peach balls in stemmed dessert dishes and spoon the sauce over peaches. 6 servings.

CRIMSON CRANBERRY FLAMBE

1 1/2 c. sugar
1 c. water
2 c. fresh cranberries

1/4 to 1/2 c. brandy
1 qt. coconut ice cream

Mix the sugar and water in a saucepan and bring to a boil, stirring until sugar is dissolved. Add the cranberries and simmer for about 5 minutes or until skins pop open. Pour into a chafing dish. Pour brandy over top and ignite. Ladle over scoops of ice cream. Six to 8 sugar cubes, soaked in lemon extract, may be substituted for brandy. 6-8 servings.

Mrs. Arthur Bone, Greenwood, Mississippi

KISMET CAKE

1 pkg. lemon cake mix	Flour
1 tsp. (scant) mace	1 c. raisins
1 1/3 c. water	1 c. chopped walnuts
2 eggs	1 whole blanched almond

Place the cake mix in a mixing bowl. Add the mace, water and eggs and mix well. Flour the raisins and walnuts lightly and fold into batter. Add the almond and mix well. Pour into a greased and floured 10-inch bundt pan. Bake at 350 degrees for about 40 minutes. Cool in pan for 10 minutes, then remove from pan. Person who gets the slice of cake with the almond will have good luck all year.

Mrs. Ed Snyder, Dothan, Alabama

ALMOND SILK PIE

1/2 c. butter or margarine	2 eggs
3/4 c. sugar	3/4 c. diced roasted almonds
1 1-oz. square unsweetened chocolate, melted	1 baked 8-in. pastry shell, cooled
1 tsp. vanilla	Whipped cream

Place the butter and sugar in a mixing bowl and beat with electric mixer until well blended. Add the chocolate, vanilla and 1 egg and beat at high speed for 5 minutes, scraping side of bowl occasionally. Add remaining egg and beat for 5 minutes longer or until light and fluffy. Stir in all except 1 tablespoon almonds. Turn into the pastry shell and chill. Cover with whipped cream and garnish with remaining almonds. 8-10 servings.

Almond Silk Pie (above)

abraham lincoln's birthday

Lincoln's Birthday is a happy holiday to be celebrating. In a very real sense, on this day we are celebrating the indomitable spirit of man — as exemplified by Lincoln — and the joys of the simpler days in which he lived.

Few presidents and heroes have been loved as Lincoln is. Born in poverty to a frontier family in Kentucky, Lincoln personified the American virtues: hard work, a love of learning, and a dream that went far beyond his childhood background. His dream came true and provided inspiration for millions of young men and women.

For your Lincoln's Birthday celebration, recall the good old days with simple and hearty foods. The menu you'll find in the beginning of this book features such dishes as Circuit Rider's Stew ... Whig's Corn Pudding ... New Salem Yams with Pecans ... and Kentucky Prune Cake. Recipes for these and many other delicious foods are in the pages that follow.

If these foods appear typical of foods served in today's South, they do so for good reason. Much of the cooking on the frontier owed a big debt to southern cuisine. Even then, people realized that the southern tradition of hospitality had given rise to another tradition, one of delicious cooking. Share in both traditions, and entertain your family and friends at a Lincoln's Birthday celebration they'll long remember.

HOT MINT TEA

1 c. (firmly packed) mint leaves	3 c. sugar
1 lge. orange pekoe tea bag	1 stick cinnamon
	Juice of 8 lge. lemons

Wash the mint leaves and place in a large saucepan. Add the tea bag, sugar, cinnamon stick and 1/2 gallon boiling water and cover. Steep for 1 hour, then strain. Add lemon juice and enough water to make 1 gallon liquid and bring to a boil. Serve hot. 16 servings.

Mrs. Thomas J. Boyd, Amarillo, Texas

SASSAFRAS TEA

3 tbsp. shaved sassafras root	Sugar
6 c. boiling water	Milk

Add sassafras shavings to boiling water in a saucepan and cover. Steep for 10 minutes. Strain and reheat until steaming hot. Serve with desired amount of sugar and milk.

Joan Paterson, Montgomery, Alabama

BLACKBERRY NECTAR

12 lb. blackberries, crushed	5 oz. tartaric acid
1 qt. boiling water	Sugar

Combine the blackberries, boiling water and tartaric acid in a large glass or earthenware container and let stand for 24 hours. Strain. Add 2 cups sugar for each cup of juice and mix well. Store in sterilized bottles or jars. Mix with desired amount of cold water and pour over ice.

Mrs. Mabel Baker, Skipperville, Alabama

RHUBARB PUNCH

3 lb. rhubarb, diced	1 c. lemon juice
2 1/3 c. sugar	3/4 c. crushed pineapple
1 1/2 c. orange juice	

Place the rhubarb in a saucepan and add 1 quart water. Bring to a boil and reduce heat. Simmer until rhubarb is soft, then strain. Add enough water to make 2 quarts liquid. Add the sugar and stir until dissolved. Add the fruit juices and pineapple and chill. Add 1 quart ice water just before serving. 1 gallon.

Mrs. James Biggers, Chattanooga, Tennessee

CAMPAIGN STEW

1 lb. coarsely ground venison	2 tbsp. catsup
Salt to taste	2 tsp. sugar
1 tsp. chili mix	1 med. onion, diced
Flour	2 med. potatoes, diced
2 tbsp. shortening	1 sm. clove of garlic,
2 qt. hot water	diced (opt.)
2 c. tomatoes	1 can kidney beans
1 tbsp. barbecue sauce	

Season the venison with salt and chili mix and dredge with flour. Cook in shortening in a heavy saucepan until browned, stirring occasionally. Add the water, tomatoes, barbecue sauce, catsup, sugar, onion, potatoes and garlic and simmer until venison is tender. Add the beans and heat through.

Mrs. Henry Helweg, Moulton, Texas

CIRCUIT RIDER'S STEW

1 hen	2 onions, chopped
Salt and pepper to taste	1 c. chopped green pepper
2 c. corn	1 c. chopped celery
4 c. tomatoes	2 c. lima beans

Place the chicken in a saucepan and cover with water. Bring to a boil and reduce heat. Simmer until chicken is tender. Remove chicken from stock and cool. Remove chicken from bones and cut in large pieces. Return to stock and add salt and pepper. Add remaining ingredients. Cook over low heat for about 2 hours, stirring occasionally.

Mrs. Ellis Fennell, Hopkinsville, Kentucky

HEARTY FRESH VEGETABLE SOUP

1 4-lb. soup bone with meat	2 carrots, quartered
2 qt. water	4 c. diced potatoes
2 tbsp. salt	1 1/2 c. sliced carrots
6 whole peppercorns	2/3 c. sliced celery
2 med. onions, quartered	1 c. cut fresh snap beans
2 sprigs of parsley	4 c. diced fresh tomatoes
2 stalks celery with leaves	

Place first 8 ingredients in a kettle and bring to a boil. Reduce heat and cover. Simmer for 2 hours. Remove soup bone and cool. Cut off meat and set aside. Strain the stock and return to kettle. Add remaining ingredients and cover. Simmer until vegetables are tender. Add the meat and serve. 10-12 servings.

Josie Leal, Seadrift, Texas

Angostura Pepperpot (below)

ANGOSTURA PEPPERPOT

2 eggs	2 potatoes, diced
Salt	2 tbsp. angostura aromatic
1 1/2 c. (about) flour	bitters
1 1/2 lb. beef chuck	2 10 1/2-oz. cans beef
1 green pepper, chopped	broth
1 onion, chopped	Pepper to taste

Beat the eggs with 1/2 teaspoon salt in a bowl until blended. Stir in enough flour to make a soft paste and knead on a heavily floured board until smooth and elastic. Roll out paper-thin and cut into 1 1/2-inch squares with a sharp knife. Place on a cloth and let dry for several hours. Cut the beef in cubes and place in a large saucepan. Cover with boiling water and cover the saucepan. Simmer for 2 hours or until beef is almost tender. Add the green pepper, onion, potatoes, angostura bitters, beef broth and 2 cups water and bring to a boil. Add the noodle squares. Cover and simmer for 15 minutes or until noodles and potatoes are tender. Season with salt to taste and pepper. 4 servings.

THRIFTY RIBS

3 lb. beef short ribs	1/4 tsp. pepper
3 tbsp. shortening	2 med. onions, sliced
1 1/2 tsp. salt	1/2 tsp. dry mustard

2 bay leaves

2 c. water

1/4 c. brown sugar

4 sm. carrots, sliced

2 c. lima beans

Flour

Brown the short ribs in shortening in a kettle and pour off drippings. Add the salt, pepper, onions, mustard, bay leaves and water and cover tightly. Cook over low heat for 2 hours. Add the sugar, carrots and beans and cook until vegetables are tender. Discard bay leaves. Place the ribs and vegetables on a warm platter. Mix enough flour with small amount of water to thicken gravy. Stir into liquid and cook, stirring, until thickened. Pour over rib mixture. 4-6 servings.

Mrs. S. A. Mahaffey, Braxton, Mississippi

ROAST WATER FOWL

2   1 1/4-lb. wild ducks

1 onion, chopped

1 garlic clove, minced

2 tbsp. unsalted butter

1 tsp. paprika

1/2 tsp. salt

1/4 tsp. hot sauce

Sliced bacon

4 c. cooked wild rice

Clean the ducks. Rub cavities with onion and garlic and leave in cavities. Combine the butter, paprika, salt and hot sauce and rub over skin of ducks. Wrap each duck in cheesecloth and place, breast down, on rack in a greased shallow pan. Roast at 325 degrees for 45 minutes to 1 hour, basting occasionally. Turn and bake for 45 minutes to 1 hour longer, basting occasionally. Remove cheesecloth and cover with strips of bacon. Bake until done and serve with wild rice. 4 servings.

Roast Water Fowl (above)

KNOB CREEK VENISON

6 slices salt pork, 1/4 in. thick	Juice of 1 lemon
1 4 to 5-lb. venison roast	2 tbsp. Worcestershire sauce
Salt and pepper to taste	1 med. onion, chopped
	1 lemon, sliced

Wash the salt pork to remove salt and place in a roasting pan in a single layer. Season the roast with salt and pepper and place on salt pork. Add lemon juice, Worcestershire sauce, onion and sliced lemon. Cover. Bake at 300 degrees until done, adding small amount of hot water, if needed. 10-12 servings.

Mrs. G. E. Rountree, Sunbury, North Carolina

HAM WITH ORANGE SAUCE

1 3/4-in. slice ham	1/2 c. water
Whole cloves	2 sweet potatoes, peeled
1 tbsp. fat	1 tbsp. cornstarch
2 tbsp. brown sugar	2 tbsp. lemon juice
1/2 c. orange juice	

Cut the ham in serving pieces and stud with cloves. Brown in fat in a pressure cooker. Add the brown sugar, orange juice and water. Cut the sweet potatoes in half and add to ham mixture. Cover the pressure cooker. Cook at 10 pounds pressure for 15 minutes. Let pressure return to normal. Mix the cornstarch with lemon juice and stir into boiling liquid. Cook for about 1 minute or until clear. 4 servings.

Mrs. Fred Brown, Durham, North Carolina

LIMA BEANS WITH SOUR CREAM

1 lb. dried lge. lima beans	1 med. onion, chopped
2 tsp. salt	1 tsp. dry mustard
1/3 c. margarine	1 c. sour cream
1 c. dark corn syrup	

Soak the beans overnight in at least 2 1/2 quarts water with 1 teaspoon salt. Drain. Rinse with hot water and drain. Melt the margarine in a large saucepan. Mix in the corn syrup and remaining salt. Add the beans and cover. Simmer for 50 to 60 minutes or until beans are tender. Stir in the onion, mustard and sour cream and turn into a 2 1/2-quart casserole. Cover. Bake at 350 degrees for 1 hour. 6 servings.

Photograph for this recipe on page 28.

English Harvest Pie (below)

ENGLISH HARVEST PIE

2 10-oz. packages frozen	2 cloves of garlic, crushed
Brussels sprouts	2 med. onions, sliced
1/3 c. all-purpose flour	1 c. sliced mushrooms
1/2 tsp. paprika	1 3/4 c. cooked carrots
1/4 tsp. rosemary	1 3/4 c. diced cooked
2 c. vegetable stock or	potatoes
bouillon	English-Herbed Pastry Shell

Cook the Brussels sprouts according to package directions and drain. Blend the flour, paprika and rosemary in a saucepan. Stir in the vegetable stock gradually and add the garlic. Cook over low heat, stirring constantly, until thickened. Add the onions, mushrooms, carrots and potatoes and cook for 5 minutes or until onions are tender, stirring occasionally. Stir in the Brussels sprouts and turn into English-Herbed Pastry Shell.

English-Herbed Pastry Shell

2 1/4 c. sifted flour	1/4 tsp. summer savory
1 1/2 tsp. salt	1/3 c. ice water
1 tsp. celery seed	1/2 c. salad oil

Sift flour and salt together into a bowl. Add the celery seed and savory and blend. Combine the water and oil. Add to the flour mixture and stir with a fork until mixture leaves side of bowl. Roll out between sheets of waxed paper to a 14-inch circle. Line a 10-inch pie plate with pastry. Trim and flute edges and prick pastry with a fork. Chill. Bake in 450-degree oven for 20 minutes and cool.

WHIG'S CORN PUDDING

2 c. corn	1/4 tsp. paprika
1/2 sm. onion, grated	1 c. milk
1/4 tsp. pepper	1 sm. green pepper, chopped
1 tsp. baking powder	1 tsp. salt
1 can pimento, chopped	2 tsp. sugar
2 eggs, well beaten	2 tbsp. melted butter

Mix all ingredients and place in a well-greased casserole. Cover. Bake in 325-degree oven for 30 minutes. Remove cover. Increase temperature to 350 degrees and bake until brown. 6 servings.

Nell Traynham, Burlington, North Carolina

NEW SALEM YAMS WITH PECANS

6 lge. yams	1/2 tsp. salt
6 tbsp. butter or margarine	3/4 c. pecan halves
3/4 c. (packed) brown sugar	

Pare the yams and cook in boiling, salted water for 15 to 20 minutes or until almost tender. Drain. Cut in halves lengthwise and place in a well-greased baking dish. Combine 3 tablespoons boiling water, butter, sugar and salt in a saucepan and boil for 3 minutes. Add pecans and pour over the potatoes. Bake in 350-degree oven for 30 minutes. 10-12 servings.

Mary B. Westerfield, Narrows, Kentucky

TURNIP GREENS

1 1-lb. ham hock	Salt to taste
3 lb. turnip greens	

Place the ham hock in a large saucepan and cover with water. Bring to a boil and reduce heat. Simmer for 20 minutes. Add the turnip greens and salt and cover. Simmer for about 45 minutes or until greens are tender.

Mrs. John Bailey, Birmingham, Alabama

BRAN BISCUITS

1/2 c. bran	1 1/2 c. flour
3/4 c. milk	2 tsp. baking powder
1/3 c. melted shortening	1 tsp. salt

Soak the bran in milk in a bowl for about 15 minutes, then stir in the shortening. Sift dry ingredients together and stir into bran mixture. Roll out on a floured board and cut with biscuit cutter. Place on a greased baking sheet. Bake at 450 degrees for 12 minutes. 8 servings.

Mrs. John Stewart, Tuscaloosa, Alabama

LIBERTY BREAD

1 1/2 c. cornmeal
1 c. cream-style corn
1 c. buttermilk
2/3 c. cooking oil
2 eggs
3 tsp. baking powder

1 tsp. salt
1 med. onion, chopped (opt.)
3 hot chili peppers, chopped
2 tsp. chopped bell pepper
1 c. grated sharp Cheddar
   cheese

Mix all ingredients except the cheese and pour half the mixture into a hot, greased skillet. Sprinkle half the cheese over cornmeal mixture and pour remaining cornmeal mixture over cheese. Top with remaining cheese. Bake at 400 degrees for 35 to 40 minutes.

Mrs. W. F. Owen, Goodlettsville, Tennessee

BAKED WALNUT BROWN BREAD

1 1/4 c. sifted flour
2 tsp. baking powder
3/4 tsp. soda
1 1/4 tsp. salt
1 1/4 c. graham flour
1 c. chopped walnuts

1 egg, lightly beaten
1/3 c. (packed) brown sugar
1/2 c. light molasses
3/4 c. buttermilk
3 tbsp. melted shortening

Sift the flour with baking powder, soda and salt into a bowl and stir in the graham flour and walnuts. Mix the egg, brown sugar, molasses, buttermilk and shortening and stir into flour mixture just until flour is moistened. Spoon into 3 greased 1-pound cans. Bake at 350 degrees for 45 minutes or until bread tests done. Let stand for 10 minutes, then turn out onto wire rack. Serve warm or cold. May be placed in a 9 x 5 x 3-inch loaf pan and baked at 350 degrees for 50 to 55 minutes.

Baked Walnut Brown Bread (above)

KENTUCKY PRUNE CAKE

1 c. oil or margarine	1 tsp. cinnamon
1 tsp. vanilla	1 tsp. ground cloves
2 c. sugar	1 tsp. allspice
1 c. buttermilk or prune juice	3 c. flour
	3 eggs
1 tsp. soda	1 c. cooked pitted prunes
1/2 tsp. salt	1 c. chopped nuts

Mix the oil, vanilla, sugar, buttermilk and soda in a bowl. Mix the salt, cinnamon, cloves, allspice and flour. Add to oil mixture and beat well. Add the eggs and mix. Chop the prunes and add to flour mixture. Add the nuts and mix well. Pour into a greased tube pan. Bake at 350 degrees for 50 minutes to 1 hour. Cool for 10 minutes and remove from pan. Cool.

Cream Cheese Frosting

1 3-oz. package cream cheese	1 box powdered sugar
6 cooked prunes, chopped	Prune juice or cream

Mix the cream cheese and prunes in a bowl. Add the sugar and enough prune juice for spreading consistency and beat until smooth. Spread on cake.

Mrs. Joseph W. Roberts, Jacksonville, Florida

PEANUT CRUNCH PIE

1/3 c. crunchy peanut butter	1/3 c. flour
3/4 c. confectioners' sugar	1/2 c. sugar
1 baked 9-in. pastry shell	1/8 tsp. salt

Peanut Crunch Pie (above)

1 tbsp. instant coffee

1 tall can evaporated milk

2 tbsp. butter

3 egg yolks, beaten

1/2 tsp. vanilla

Blend the peanut butter with confectioners' sugar until mixture resembles coarse meal. Spread 2/3 of the mixture in bottom of the pastry shell. Combine the flour, sugar, salt and coffee in a medium saucepan and stir in the milk. Add the butter and cook over medium heat, stirring constantly, until thickened. Remove from heat. Stir 1/3 of the milk mixture into egg yolks gradually, then stir back into milk mixture in saucepan. Bring to a boil, stirring constantly, and remove from heat. Stir in the vanilla. Pour over peanut butter mixture in pastry shell and sprinkle with remaining peanut butter mixture. Cool, then chill.

PECAN-SOUR CREAM PIE

1 recipe pie pastry

1 c. chopped pecans

2 tsp. flour

1/4 tsp. cinnamon

1/4 tsp. cloves

1 c. sour cream

2 eggs, well beaten

1 c. sugar

1/2 tsp. grated lemon rind

Whipped cream

Line a pie plate with pastry and sprinkle with pecans. Mix the flour, cinnamon, cloves and small amount of sour cream, then add remaining sour cream gradually. Stir in the eggs, sugar and lemon rind and pour into pie shell. Bake in 450-degree oven for 10 minutes. Reduce temperature to 325 degrees and bake for about 40 minutes longer or until firm. Serve with whipped cream.

Mrs. W. L. Alverson, Fairfield, Alabama

COTTAGE PUDDING WITH BLUEBERRY SAUCE

1/4 c. shortening

1 c. sugar

1 egg

1/4 tsp. lemon extract

1 3/4 c. all-purpose flour

2 1/2 tsp. baking powder

1/2 tsp. salt

1/2 tsp. nutmeg

1/2 tsp. cinnamon

2/3 c. milk

1 No. 2 can blueberry pie

filling

1/4 c. honey

1/4 c. butter

3 tbsp. lemon juice

Cream the shortening and sugar in a bowl. Add the egg and lemon extract and beat well. Sift the flour, baking powder, salt and spices together and add to creamed mixture alternately with milk, beating well after each addition. Pour into a waxed paper-lined 8 x 8 x 2-inch pan. Bake in 350-degree oven for 35 minutes or until done, then cut into squares. Combine the pie filling, honey, butter and lemon juice in a saucepan and heat through. Spoon over warm pudding squares.

Hazel Wimer, Hightown, Virginia

Cherry Bavarian Valentine (page 50)

st. valentine's day

In Victorian times when a young man was courting a girl, the flowers he sent her on St. Valentine's Day had a language of their own. Every girl held her breath, hoping for white roses — which meant "I love you." Today, the language of flowers has all but disappeared. Our lives are too fast paced for the leisurely niceties of by-gone times. But St. Valentine's Day is still the time for telling the people we love how special they are. Whether the man in your life is a favorite beau or your husband of many years, he still looks forward to Valentine's Day. This year, why not make this romantic day a real occasion with the delicious menu you'll find in the beginning of your book.

From kitchens all over the South have come recipes *Southern Living* readers have depended upon when they wanted to serve the mouth-watering foods necessary for a memorable meal. Some of the foods are especially southern — Beaten Biscuits with Lemon Butter Balls, for example. Others, such as Asparagus Salad with Beet Hearts, are universal favorites.

These are just some of the recipes you'll find in the pages that follow. Every one is the home-tested favorite of a woman who takes pride in her skill as a good cook. As you browse through this section, imagine yourself creating a St. Valentine's menu that says "I love you" — in your own unique language.

41

PINK SILK PUNCH

1 c. sugar syrup	1 qt. fresh strawberries,
6 thin slices orange	crushed
6 thin slices lemon	1/4 c. maraschino cherry
1 tbsp. grated lemon rind	juice
1 tbsp. grated orange rind	1 qt. pink lemonade
1 tsp. angostura bitters	1 qt. carbonated water

Combine all ingredients in order listed. Place in a punch bowl and add large piece of ice. Sugar syrup may be made by mixing equal parts of sugar and water and boiling for 10 minutes. Store unused portion in refrigerator. 3-4 quarts.

Mrs. Marie James, Pascagoula, Mississippi

SWEETHEART CHIFFON LEMONADE

Juice of 12 lge. lemons	1 qt. water
2 c. sugar	Red food coloring
1 qt. carbonated water	

Mix the lemon juice and sugar, then stir into the carbonated water slowly. Add 2 cups cracked ice and stir. Add the water and enough food coloring for desired shade. Serve in frosted glasses. 8 servings.

Mrs. Alfred Mayhand, Little Rock, Arkansas

SHRIMP BISQUE

1/4 c. butter	1 qt. milk
1 sm. onion, chopped	1 1/2 tsp. salt
1/2 c. finely diced celery	1/2 tsp. hot sauce
1 lb. fresh shelled shrimp,	1/4 tsp. paprika
chopped	2 tsp. lemon juice
2 tbsp. flour	

Melt the butter in a large saucepan. Add the onion and celery and cook until onion is tender. Add the shrimp and cook for 2 minutes, stirring frequently. Blend in the flour and stir in milk gradually. Add the seasonings and lemon juice and bring to a boil. Reduce heat and simmer for 5 minutes. Canned or cooked crab or lobster may be substituted for shrimp. 4-6 servings.

Henrietta Miller, Sarasota, Florida

RED VELVET SOUP WITH CROUTON HEARTS

1 qt. tomato juice	**1 can evaporated milk**
1 stick margarine	**Crouton Hearts**

Combine the tomato juice and margarine in a saucepan and bring to a boil. Remove from heat. Add the milk slowly, stirring constantly. Keep warm but do not boil. Serve in bowls and sprinkle with Crouton Hearts.

Crouton Hearts

6 slices bread	**Garlic-flavored butter**

Cut slices of bread with small heart-shaped cookie cutter. Spread with butter and place on a baking sheet. Bake in a 300-degree oven until dry.

Mrs. Dulane O. Holt, Sanford, North Carolina

VICHYSSOISE

2 c. diced potatoes	**2 tbsp. finely chopped**
1 qt. chicken stock	**parsley**
1 pt. cream	**1 tbsp. flour**
1 onion, minced	**1 tsp. salt**
4 tbsp. butter	**Pepper to taste**

Place the potatoes and chicken stock in a saucepan and bring to a boil. Reduce heat and simmer until potatoes are tender. Drain and reserve stock. Rice the potatoes. Heat the cream and onion in a double boiler. Saute the parsley in butter for 1 minute, then stir in flour. Stir into cream mixture. Stir in potatoes and cook for 3 minutes. Add salt and pepper. 4 servings.

Nell Criswell, Justin, Texas

JELLIED CHICKEN SALAD

1 1/2 tbsp. unflavored gelatin	**1 tbsp. lemon juice**
1/4 c. cold water	**1 c. chopped cooked chicken**
1 c. consomme, heated	**1 c. cooked peas**
1 tbsp. chopped onion	**2 tbsp. chopped celery**
Salt to taste	**2 tbsp. chopped pickle**

Soften the gelatin in water, then dissolve in consomme. Stir in the onion, salt and lemon juice and chill until slightly thickened. Stir in the chicken, peas, celery and pickle and pour into individual molds. Chill until firm. Unmold and serve on lettuce. 4-6 servings.

Mrs. Charles Quinn, Fort Worth, Texas

PINK CHAMPAGNE-FRUIT SALAD

1 env. unflavored gelatin	1/2 c. diced pineapple
1 tbsp. sugar	1 c. sliced seedless grapes
Dash of salt	1/2 c. diced celery
1 tbsp. lemon juice	1/2 c. chopped pecans
1/2 c. pink champagne	1/2 c. whipped cream

Soften the gelatin in 2 tablespoons cold water. Add 1/2 cup boiling water and stir until gelatin is dissolved. Add the sugar, salt, lemon juice and champagne and mix well. Chill until slightly thickened. Fold in fruits, celery, pecans and whipped cream and chill until firm. 6-8 servings.

Maggie Johnson, Varnado, Louisiana

ASPARAGUS SALAD WITH BEET HEARTS

3/4 c. sugar	2 chopped pimentos
1 c. water	1 can cut asparagus, drained
1/2 c. white vinegar	Juice of 1/2 lemon
2 env. unflavored gelatin	2 tsp. grated onion
1/2 tsp. salt	Lettuce or watercress
1 c. chopped celery	Beet Hearts
1/2 c. chopped pecans	

Mix the sugar, water and vinegar in a saucepan and bring to a boil. Dissolve the gelatin in 1/2 cup water. Add to vinegar mixture and stir until dissolved. Add remaining ingredients except lettuce and beets, then cool. Pour into a mold and chill until firm. Unmold on lettuce and surround with Beet Hearts.

Beet Hearts

6 tbsp. salad oil	1/4 tsp. sugar
4 tbsp. wine vinegar	1 lge. can sliced beets

Combine the oil, vinegar and sugar in a small mixing bowl. Drain the beets and cut the slices into heart shapes with a cookie cutter. Place beet hearts in the vinegar mixture and marinate in refrigerator for about 1 hour, basting occasionally. Drain.

Mrs. Burton M. Newell, Sr., Greensboro, North Carolina

TOMATO AND RELISH ASPIC

1 tbsp. unflavored gelatin	1 can tomato soup
1/2 c. cold water	2 tbsp. tarragon vinegar
1/3 c. sugar	2 tbsp. lemon juice
1 tsp. salt	1/4 tsp. celery salt

1 c. sliced stuffed olives
1 sm. onion, grated
1 sm. green pepper, chopped

1 cucumber, finely chopped
1/2 c. chopped pecans

Soften the gelatin in cold water for 5 minutes. Add the sugar and salt to soup in a saucepan and bring to a boil. Add the gelatin and stir until dissolved. Add vinegar, lemon juice and celery salt and stir until mixed. Chill until thickened. Stir in remaining ingredients and pour into a heart-shaped mold. Chill until firm. 8-10 servings.

Lela A. Tomlinson, Baton Rouge, Louisiana

VALENTINE ASPICS

2 env. unflavored gelatin
3 1/2 c. tomato juice
3/4 tsp. hot sauce
1/2 tsp. salt
1 tsp. sugar
1 tsp. Worcestershire sauce
1/4 c. lemon or lime juice

8 bread slices
6 stuffed olives, finely
  chopped
1 3-oz. package cream
  cheese
1 c. mayonnaise

Soften the gelatin in 1 cup tomato juice in a saucepan. Place over low heat, stirring constantly, until gelatin is dissolved. Remove from heat and stir in remaining tomato juice, 1/4 teaspoon hot sauce, salt, sugar, Worcestershire sauce and lemon juice. Pour into 8 individual heart-shaped molds and chill until firm. Cut bread slices into heart shapes the same size as molds. Add the olives to cream cheese and blend well. Spread on bread. Unmold aspic on cream cheese-topped bread. Mix the mayonnaise with remaining hot sauce and serve with salads. 8 servings.

Valentine Aspics (above)

Jambalaya (below)

JAMBALAYA

3 c. water	1/2 c. chopped onion
2 tsp. salt	1/2 c. chopped green pepper
1 tsp. hot sauce	1 garlic clove, minced
1 bay leaf	1 c. rice
1 stalk celery with leaves	1 1-lb. can tomatoes
1 lb. shrimp	3/4 c. bouillon
1/4 c. butter or margarine	1 1/2 c. diced cooked ham

Mix the water, 1 teaspoon salt and 1/2 teaspoon hot sauce in a saucepan. Add the bay leaf and celery and bring to a boil. Add the shrimp. Bring to a boil and cook for 5 minutes. Drain the shrimp and cool quickly. Shell and clean. Melt the butter in a large skillet. Add the onion, green pepper and garlic and cook until onion is tender but not brown. Stir in the rice, tomatoes, bouillon and remaining salt and hot sauce. Bring to a boil and reduce heat. Cover the skillet and simmer for 20 minutes. Add the ham and shrimp and cover. Cook for 10 minutes longer or until liquid is absorbed. 4-6 servings.

CORNISH HENS WITH PARSLEY SAUCE

3 Rock Cornish hens	Pinch of dried thyme
4 tbsp. flour	Pinch of dried sage
4 tsp. salt	3/4 tsp. chili powder
1 tsp. pepper	3/4 tsp. paprika
6 tbsp. butter	2 tbsp. sherry
Pinch of dried marjoram	1 c. chopped parsley

Cut the hens in half. Combine the flour, salt and pepper in a paper bag. Add the hens and shake to coat evenly. Melt the butter in a Dutch oven and stir in marjoram, thyme, sage, chili powder and paprika. Add the hens, several halves at a time, and brown. Place all halves in the Dutch oven and cover tightly. Cook over low heat until fork-tender. Place on a heated platter and keep warm. Pour the sherry into the Dutch oven and stir to loosen browned particles. Add the parsley and cook for 2 minutes. Pour over hens. One-fourth cup white wine may be substituted for sherry. 6 servings.

Mrs. Phillip Russell, Jonesboro, Georgia

BAKED SNAPPER WITH RED SAUCE

1/4 c. shortening	1 c. water
1/4 c. flour	1 tbsp. vinegar
1/4 c. finely chopped onion	1 tsp. sugar
1/2 c. finely chopped celery	1 stick butter or margarine
1 sm. can tomato sauce	1 red snapper

Melt the shortening in a saucepan and stir in flour. Add the onion and celery and cook over low heat for about 10 minutes. Stir in the tomato sauce, water, vinegar and sugar. Melt the butter. Place the snapper in a shallow baking pan and pour butter over snapper. Pour tomato sauce mixture over snapper. Bake at 350 degrees until snapper is done.

Mrs. Robert S. Talbot, Cantonment, Florida

BUTTERFLY SHRIMP

1 lb. fresh jumbo shrimp	3/4 tsp. baking powder
3 tbsp. flour	3/4 tsp. salt
1 1/2 tbsp. cornstarch	1/2 c. milk
1 tbsp. white cornmeal	

Peel the shrimp, leaving tails on. Cut a deep slit along the back and remove the black veins. Open cut portion and press shrimp flat. Mix the flour, cornstarch, cornmeal, baking powder and salt in a bowl. Add the milk and mix well. Dip each shrimp in batter and fry in deep fat at 375 degrees for 2 to 3 minutes or until golden brown.

Sauce

1/4 c. soy sauce	1/8 tsp. pepper
2 tbsp. honey	1 clove of garlic, minced
1/2 tsp. salt	

Mix the soy sauce, honey, salt, pepper and garlic in a saucepan and heat through. Serve with shrimp. 4 servings.

Mrs. Mary Costello, Prattville, Alabama

Elegant Ripe Olive-Onion Tarts (below)

ELEGANT RIPE OLIVE-ONION TARTS

1 1/2 c. canned pitted ripe
   olives
1 1/2 c. thinly sliced onions
2 tbsp. butter
1/2 tsp. garlic salt
1/4 tsp. salt
1/8 tsp. white pepper

2 eggs, beaten
1/2 c. half and half
8 unbaked 3 1/2-in. tart
   shells
1 tbsp. grated Parmesan
   cheese

Preheat oven to 375 degrees. Drain the olives and cut in large pieces. Cook the onions in butter in a saucepan over low heat until soft but not browned. Cool. Add the olives, seasonings, eggs and half and half and mix well. Spoon into tart shells and sprinkle with Parmesan cheese. Place on a baking sheet and place on rack in lower half of oven. Bake for 20 to 25 minutes or until pastry is browned and filling is set. Serve warm. 8 servings.

GREEN ONIONS WITH ANCHOVY BUTTER

36 green onions
6 buttered toast rounds
2 tsp. chopped parsley
Juice of 1 lemon
2 hard-boiled egg yolks,
   chopped

2 tbsp. soft butter
2 tbsp. finely chopped
   watercress
Anchovy paste to taste
1/2 c. soft bread crumbs

Wash the green onions and trim the stalks to 4 inches. Place in a large skillet in 1/4 inch water and bring to a boil. Cover the skillet tightly and cook for about 6 minutes or until onions are just tender. Stack 6 onions on each toast round. Sprinkle the onions with parsley, lemon juice and egg yolks. Mix the butter and watercress in a skillet and stir in the anchovy paste. Add the bread crumbs and cook over low heat until brown, stirring constantly. Sprinkle over the onions.

Mrs. Evelyn Boswell, Miami, Florida

ARTICHOKES WITH DESERT SLAW

6 artichokes
2 tsp. salt
1 c. (firmly packed) shredded
   carrots
1/3 c. chopped radishes
1 1/2 c. (firmly packed)
   shredded red cabbage
1/4 c. sliced stuffed olives

1/4 c. chopped parsley
1/4 c. olive or salad oil
2 tbsp. vinegar
Dash of pepper
1 tsp. sugar
1 clove of garlic, minced
Mayonnaise

Wash the artichokes and cut stems off evenly at base so artichokes will stand. Remove small bottom leaves. Trim prickly tips off the remaining leaves and cut about 1 inch off top of each artichoke. Stand artichokes upright in a deep saucepan or Dutch oven. Add 1 1/2 teaspoons salt and 2 to 3 inches of boiling water and cover. Simmer for 35 to 45 minutes or until a leaf may be pulled off without effort, adding boiling water if needed. Turn artichokes upside down to drain. Spread leaves apart gently and remove choke from the cavity with a metal spoon. Chill. Combine the carrots, radishes, cabbage, olives and parsley in a large bowl. Blend remaining salt and remaining ingredients except mayonnaise. Pour over cabbage mixture and toss lightly to blend. Cover and chill for several hours. Drain. Fill each artichoke with slaw and serve with mayonnaise.

Artichokes with Desert Slaw (above)

BEATEN BISCUITS WITH LEMON-BUTTER

2 c. self-rising flour	1/4 c. shortening
1 tbsp. sugar	2/3 c. water

Mix the flour and sugar in a mixing bowl and cut in shortening until mixture resembles cornmeal. Add the water, small amount at a time, to make a stiff dough. Turn out onto lightly floured surface and knead. Beat with small mallet for 4 minutes. Roll out to 1 inch thickness and cut with 2-inch biscuit cutter. Place on ungreased cookie sheet. Bake at 400 degrees until lightly browned.

Lemon-Butter Balls

1 c. butter	Minced parsley
1/4 c. lemon juice	

Cream the butter and lemon juice in a bowl, then chill. Shape into small balls, using about 2 teaspoons for each, and roll the balls in parsley. Serve with biscuits.

Mrs. Lester Harris, Muskogee, Oklahoma

CHERRY BAVARIAN VALENTINE

2 env. unflavored gelatin	1 1/4 c. milk
1 tsp. ginger	Red food coloring (opt.)
1/4 tsp. salt	1/2 c. sugar
1 8-oz. jar red maraschino	2 c. heavy cream, whipped
cherries	Whole or halved maraschino
6 eggs, separated	cherries

Mix the gelatin, ginger and salt in top of a double boiler. Drain the cherries and reserve syrup. Add enough water to reserved syrup to make 3/4 cup liquid and stir into gelatin mixture. Add beaten egg yolks and milk and blend thoroughly. Cook over boiling water, stirring constantly, until gelatin is dissolved and mixture is thickened. Remove from heat and chill until partially set. Chop the cherries and stir into gelatin mixture. Stir in several drops of food coloring. Beat the egg whites in a bowl until soft peaks form. Beat until stiff, adding sugar gradually, then fold into the cherry mixture. Reserve 3/4 cup whipped cream and fold remaining whipped cream into cherry mixture. Turn into a 10-cup heart-shaped mold and chill for 4 hours or overnight. Unmold onto serving plate and outline top of heart shape with whole cherries. Force reserved whipped cream through star tube in cake decorator to make lace fluting around cherry heart. 10-12 servings.

Photograph for this recipe on page 40.

FRUIT FLAMBE LOVING CUP

4 tbsp. butter	1 c. sliced strawberries
2 pears, peeled	1 banana, sliced
1/2 c. diced pineapple	1 c. apricot puree

1/2 c. heated rum   Pink-tinted whipped cream
Ladyfingers

Melt the butter in a chafing dish over a flame. Core and slice the pears and place in the chafing dish. Add the pineapple, strawberries and banana and cook until fruits are heated. Add the puree and cook for 1 minute longer. Pour rum over fruits and ignite. Serve over ladyfingers and top with whipped cream.

Mrs. Al Skinner, Silver City, New Mexico

CHERRY BOUGH CAKE

1 15-oz. package angel   White Snow Frosting
    food cake mix   1 1/3 c. flaked coconut
1/4 c. chopped drained   Red food coloring
    maraschino cherries

Prepare the angel food cake mix according to package directions and fold in the cherries. Place in a 10-inch tube pan. Bake according to package directions. Invert pan and cool. Remove cake from pan and spread with White Snow Frosting. Tint coconut a pale pink with food coloring and sprinkle over side of cake. Garnish with stemmed whole maraschino cherries.

White Snow Frosting

2 egg whites   1/3 c. water
1 1/2 c. sugar   2 tsp. light corn syrup
Dash of salt

Combine all ingredients in top of a double boiler and beat well with rotary beater or electric mixer. Place over boiling water and cook, beating constantly, for 7 minutes or until frosting holds soft peaks. Remove from boiling water and beat until frosting holds stiff peaks.

Cherry Bough Cake (above)

Cherry-Apple Dumplings (page 60)

george washington's birthday

The Southland is famous not just for its hospitality and cuisine but for the national leaders it has produced — men like Jefferson, Washington, and Madison who were instrumental in transforming a group of colonies into a thriving and independent nation. Of all Southerners who contributed to our country's beginnings, none is more remembered than George Washington, "the father of our country."

As a southern gentleman and a plantation owner, George Washington enjoyed the "good life" of fine foods. He was a gracious host, too, following the tradition of his native Virginia. Once he wrote to a friend that, the previous evening, "for the first time in twenty years, Mrs. Washington and I sat down to dinner alone."

Both the tradition of hospitality personified by George and Martha Washington and the cherry tree legend so much a part of folklore about our first president provide the themes for the Washington's Birthday menu in the front of this book. And on the next pages, you'll discover recipes for traditional foods such as Little Hunting Creek Doves . . . Senators' Bean Soup (still served in Washington on Capitol Hill) . . . Mount Vernon Steamed Pudding . . . and every kind of food you might want to serve your family and guests on Washington's Birthday. These foods have been tried and proven in hundreds of southern homes and are now awaiting their turn in yours!

RATIFICATION PUNCH

1 qt. cherry soda	**Peel of 1/2 orange**
14 whole cloves	**2 tbsp. sugar**
Peel of 1 lime or lemon	**1 stick cinnamon**

Combine all ingredients in the top of a double boiler and place over boiling water. Cook, stirring constantly, for 15 minutes, but do not boil. Strain and serve in demitasse cups with dessert. 12 servings.

Gladys Farmer, Warrenton, North Carolina

TIDEWATER TEA

1 qt. strong tea	**Juice of 1 orange**
1 c. Bing cherry juice	**4 whole cloves**
Juice of 1 lemon	**1 stick cinnamon**

Combine all the ingredients in a saucepan. Bring to a boil and reduce heat. Simmer for 10 minutes and remove from heat. Strain and serve. 4 servings.

Mrs. H. J. Rice, Waco, Texas

SENATOR'S BEAN SOUP

2 c. dried navy beans	**1 c. finely diced potatoes**
1 c. diced salt pork	**Salt and pepper to taste**
1/2 c. chopped onion	**1 c. milk or evaporated**
1 carrot, thinly sliced	**milk (opt.)**

Pick over the beans, discarding any that are discolored, and wash in cold water. Drain. Cover with water and soak overnight. Drain. Cook pork in heavy kettle over moderate heat until golden brown. Add the onion and cook until transparent but not brown. Add the beans and enough cold water to cover and bring to a boil. Reduce heat and cover. Simmer for 2 hours. Add the carrot and potatoes and cook for 30 minutes longer. Season with salt and pepper and add the milk. Bring to a boil and serve. 6 servings.

Mrs. E. E. Bradford, Stephenville, Texas

BARLEY BROTH

2 lb. lamb neck or breast	**6 whole peppercorns**
1/2 c. pearl barley	**2 qt. water**
Salt	**3/4 c. chopped onion**

3/4 c. chopped celery
3/4 c. diced turnips
3/4 c. diced carrots
1 carrot, grated

1 c. cooked peas
2 tbsp. minced parsley
Pepper to taste

Place the lamb, barley, 1 teaspoon salt and peppercorns in a large kettle and add the water. Simmer for about 1 hour and 30 minutes, then cool and skim. Remove lamb. Remove lamb from bones and discard fat. Dice the lamb and place in kettle. Add the onion, celery, turnips and diced carrots and bring to a boil. Simmer for 30 minutes or until vegetables are tender. Add grated carrot, peas, parsley, salt to taste and pepper just before serving. 4-6 servings.

Valorie S. Jensen, Elko, Nevada

BROCCOLI CHOWDER

2 lb. fresh broccoli
2 12 1/2-oz. cans chicken
  broth
3 c. milk
1 c. chopped cooked ham
2 tsp. salt

1/4 tsp. pepper
1 c. light cream
1/2 lb. Swiss cheese,
  grated
1/4 c. butter

Place the broccoli in a large kettle and add 1 can chicken broth. Bring to a boil and reduce heat. Cover and simmer for about 7 minutes or until just tender. Remove broccoli and broth and cool. Chop coarsely. Add remaining chicken broth, milk, ham, salt and pepper to broth in kettle and bring to a boil over medium heat, stirring occasionally. Stir in remaining ingredients and broccoli and heat to serving temperature. About 2 1/2 quarts.

Broccoli Chowder (above)

Clam-Cottage Cheese Mold (below)

CLAM-COTTAGE CHEESE MOLD

1 8-oz. can minced clams	3 or 4 drops of hot sauce
1 env. unflavored gelatin	Dash of grated nutmeg
1 1/4 c. skim milk	2/3 c. cottage cheese
1/2 tsp. Worcestershire sauce	1 tbsp. chopped green pepper
1/2 tsp. salt	1/2 tbsp. onion flakes

Drain the clams and reserve 1/2 cup liquid. Mix the gelatin with reserved clam liquid in a saucepan. Place over low heat and stir for 3 minutes or until gelatin is dissolved. Remove from heat and add the milk, Worcestershire sauce, salt, hot sauce and nutmeg. Chill until mixture is consistency of unbeaten egg whites. Add the clams, cottage cheese, green pepper and onion flakes and turn into a 2 1/2-cup mold or small loaf pan. Chill until firm. Unmold to serve. 3 servings.

CHERRY TOMATOES VINAIGRETTE

2 c. cherry tomatoes, halved	1/4 c. wine vinegar
1 lge. cucumber, thinly sliced	1/2 tsp. garlic salt
2 tbsp. chopped parsley	1/4 tsp. ground savory
1 lge. onion, sliced	1/4 tsp. celery salt
in rings	1/4 tsp. crumbled tarragon
1/2 c. salad oil	1/4 tsp. pepper
1/4 tsp. salt	1 crumbled bay leaf

Layer the tomatoes, cucumber, parsley and onion rings in a shallow dish. Blend remaining ingredients and pour over vegetables. Cover and chill overnight. Drain and serve. 4-5 servings.

Mary Elizabeth Kloos, Panama City, Florida

CHERRY SUPREME SALAD

1 lge. can dark pitted
   cherries
2 pkg. black cherry gelatin
3 c. boiling water

1/2 c. sherry
1 pkg. cream cheese
1 c. chopped pecans

Drain the cherries and reserve juice. Add the gelatin to boiling water and stir until dissolved. Cool, then stir in reserved cherry juice and sherry. Chill until thickened. Stuff the cherries with cream cheese. Mix the pecans with remaining cream cheese and shape into balls. Add cherries and cheese balls to the gelatin and pour into a mold. Chill until firm.

Mrs. Lynda B. Winburn, Atlanta, Georgia

ROYAL ALMOND-CHERRY RING

2 3-oz. packages cherry
   gelatin
1/2 c. sugar
1/4 tsp. salt
1 No. 2 can Bing cherries

1/4 c. lemon juice
1/2 c. almond or pecan
   halves (opt.)
Salad greens
2 c. cottage cheese

Mix the gelatin, sugar and salt in a bowl. Drain the cherries and add enough water to cherry juice to make 3 1/4 cups liquid. Pour into a saucepan and heat to boiling point. Add gelatin mixture and stir until dissolved. Stir in lemon juice and chill until partially set. Fold in cherries and almonds and pour into a 2-quart ring mold. Chill until firm. Unmold on greens and fill center with cottage cheese. Garnish with mint. 8 servings.

Mrs. Roy D. Ireland, Shepherdsville, Kentucky

LAFAYETTE MEAT PIE

1/2 lb. ground pork
2 lb. ground beef
1 med. onion, minced
1 med. potato, cut in cubes
2 1/2 tsp. salt
1/4 tsp. pepper
3/4 tsp. allspice

1/2 tsp. cloves
1/4 tsp. sage
3/4 tsp. poultry seasoning
1/4 tsp. garlic powder
2 c. flour
2/3 c. lard

Place the meats and onion in a heavy skillet and cook over low heat, stirring, until brown. Add the potato, 2 teaspoons salt and remaining seasonings and stir well. Add 1 cup water. Simmer for 30 minutes or until most of the liquid has evaporated, then cool. Place the flour and remaining salt in a bowl and cut in lard with pastry blender. Stir in enough water to hold ingredients together. Roll out half the pastry and place in a pie plate. Add the meat mixture. Roll out remaining pastry and place on top. Cut slits in middle of pastry. Bake at 450 degrees for 10 minutes. Reduce temperature to 350 degrees and bake for 30 minutes longer or until golden brown. 6-8 servings.

Mrs. Marlene Couvrechal, Montgomery, Alabama

PORK ROAST MARASCHINO

1 tbsp. salad oil	5 tsp. cornstarch
2 cloves of garlic	2 tbsp. cold water
1 29 1/2-oz. can pineapple chunks	1 tbsp. soy sauce
1 c. sweet mixed pickles	2 tsp. salt
1 16-oz. jar maraschino cherries	1 4 to 5-lb. pork loin roast

Heat the oil in a saucepan. Add the garlic and saute for several minutes. Remove garlic and discard. Drain the pineapple, pickles and cherries, reserving 2 cups combined liquid. Blend the cornstarch with cold water and stir in reserved liquid, soy sauce and salt. Add to oil in saucepan and cook, stirring, until thickened. Set glaze aside. Place the roast on rack in a shallow roasting pan. Bake in 325-degree oven for 35 to 45 minutes per pound or until meat thermometer registers 170 degrees, basting with part of the glaze during last 1 hour and 30 minutes of baking. Place the roast on a serving platter. Add fruits and pickles to remaining glaze and heat through. Pour over the roast. 6-8 servings.

VIRGINIA ROAST PORK WITH CHERRY GLAZE

1 3 to 4-lb. pork loin roast	2 c. cider
Whole cloves	Cherry preserves
1 1/2 tsp. salt	Flour
1/2 tsp. pepper	3/4 c. chicken broth or water

Score the fat on pork and stud with cloves. Mix 1 teaspoon salt and 1/4 teaspoon pepper and sprinkle on pork. Place in a baking pan. Roast at 350 degrees for 1 hour and 45 minutes to 2 hours and 15 minutes, basting occasionally with cider. Spread thin layer of cherry preserves over the pork and roast for 20 minutes longer. Drain off fat into a saucepan and stir in small amount of flour. Add the broth and cook, stirring, until thickened. Add remaining salt and pepper and serve with pork. Add remaining seasonings. 8 servings.

Mrs. T. H. Suddath, Norfolk, Virginia

LITTLE HUNTING CREEK DOVE

14 to 16 dove	1/2 c. chopped onion
Salt and pepper to taste	1 1/2 c. water
Flour	1 c. sherry
1/2 c. salad oil	1/4 c. chopped parsley

Season the dove with salt and pepper and dredge with flour. Brown in oil in a skillet, then place in a heavy roaster. Add the onion, water and sherry and cover. Bake at 350 degrees until dove are tender, basting occasionally. Add the parsley and serve.

Mrs. Harriet Lard, Maringouin, Louisiana

Pork Roast Maraschino (page 58)

BRANDYWINE BEEF

1 6-lb. rolled boneless sirloin tip, or rump roast	1 tsp. marjoram
1 c. wine vinegar	1 tsp. crushed dried red pepper
1/2 c. olive or salad oil	1 tsp. salt
3 tbsp. lemon juice	1 clove of garlic, minced
2 tsp. thyme	1 bay leaf

Place the roast in a large, shallow pan. Mix remaining ingredients and pour over roast. Cover and chill for 3 to 4 hours, turning roast occasionally. Drain and reserve marinade. Place the roast in a baking pan. Roast at 325 degrees until done, basting occasionally with reserved marinade. 12 servings.

Mrs. M. H. Webber, Seabrook, Texas

SOUTHERN CORNMEAL ROLLS

1 1/2 c. flour	1 tbsp. sugar
3/4 c. cornmeal	4 tbsp. melted shortening
3 tsp. baking powder	1 egg, beaten
1/4 tsp. soda	1/2 c. buttermilk
1 tsp. salt	Melted butter

Sift the dry ingredients together into a bowl. Combine the shortening, egg and buttermilk. Add to dry ingredients and mix well. Roll out on lightly floured board and cut with biscuit cutter. Brush with melted butter and fold as for Parker House rolls. Place on a greased baking sheet. Bake at 450 degrees for 12 to 15 minutes.

Mrs. A. M. Boom, Memphis, Tennessee

CHERRY-APPLE DUMPLINGS

2 2/3 c. sifted all-purpose flour	1/3 c. (firmly packed) light brown sugar
1 1/4 tsp. salt	3/4 tsp. cinnamon
1 c. vegetable shortening	6 med. tart apples
1 8-oz. jar red maraschino cherries	Cream or milk
1/3 c. finely chopped walnuts	1 1/8 c. sugar

Combine the flour and salt in a bowl and cut in the shortening until mixture resembles coarse meal. Sprinkle with 6 1/2 tablespoons water and toss with a fork until mixed. Press into a ball. Roll out on a lightly floured surface to a 14 x 21-inch rectangle and cut into six 7-inch squares. Drain the cherries and reserve syrup. Reserve half the cherries. Chop remaining cherries coarsely and drain on paper towels. Combine with walnuts, brown sugar and 1/4 teaspoon cinnamon. Pare and core the apples. Place an apple on each pastry square and fill cavity with cherry mixture. Moisten edges of square with cream. Bring opposite corners of pastry up over apple and press together. Repeat with remaining corners and brush dumplings with cream. Blend 2 tablespoons sugar with remaining cinnamon and sprinkle over dumplings. Place dumplings on ungreased baking sheet. Bake in 400-degree oven for 30 to 35 minutes or until browned. Spread remaining sugar evenly over bottom of a large saucepan. Place over low heat and let stand undisturbed until sugar melts and forms a light golden brown liquid. Mix 3/4 cup water and 1/4 cup reserved cherry syrup in a saucepan and bring to a boil. Add to caramelized sugar very slowly, stirring constantly, and cook, stirring, until clear and thick. Add reserved cherries and serve warm or cold with dumplings.

Photograph for this recipe on page 52.

MT. VERNON STEAMED PUDDING

2 1/2 c. sifted flour	1 c. pitted cherries, drained
1/2 tsp. salt	1 c. cherry juice
4 tsp. baking powder	1 c. water
1/3 c. shortening	1 tbsp. cornstarch
1 2/3 c. sugar	3 tbsp. butter
1 egg	1/2 tsp. red food coloring
1 c. milk	

Sift the flour, salt and baking powder together. Cream the shortening and 2/3 cup sugar in a bowl. Add the egg and beat well. Add the milk and dry ingredients alternately, beating well after each addition. Add the cherries and blend thoroughly. Pour into a greased mold and cover. Place on a rack in a kettle with 2 inches of boiling water and steam for 2 hours, adding water as needed. Combine the cherry juice, remaining sugar, water and cornstarch in a saucepan and cook until thick, stirring constantly. Stir in the butter and food coloring and serve with pudding. 8-10 servings.

Mrs. William McLean Smith, Springville, Alabama

BLACK FOREST CAKE

1/2 c. butter or margarine
1 c. sugar
6 eggs, separated, at room
   temperature
4 1-oz. squares semisweet
   chocolate, melted
   and cooled
Kirsch
1 1/2 c. grated toasted
   filberts

1/4 c. unsifted all-purpose
   flour
1 1-lb. jar red maraschino
   cherries
1 1/2 tbsp. cornstarch
1 tbsp. lemon juice
3 c. heavy cream
1/3 c. sifted confectioners'
   sugar
Chocolate curls

Cream the butter and sugar in a bowl and beat in egg yolks, one at a time. Blend in melted chocolate and 2 tablespoons kirsch. Mix the filberts and flour and stir into butter mixture. Beat the egg whites until stiff but not dry and fold into flour mixture. Turn into a greased and floured 8-inch springform pan. Bake in 375-degree oven for 1 hour or until cake tests done. Cake may have slight crack. Cool for 10 minutes in pan. Remove from pan and cool thoroughly on cake rack. Drain the maraschino cherries and reserve syrup and 13 cherries. Slice remaining cherries. Combine reserved cherry syrup and enough kirsch to make 3/4 cup liquid and blend into cornstarch in a saucepan gradually. Add lemon juice and stir over medium heat for 30 seconds or until mixture boils. Add sliced cherries and cool. Cut cake into 3 layers with a long, sharp knife. Place top layer inverted on cake platter and spread with 1/2 of the cherry filling. Whip the cream in a large bowl with electric mixer until stiff, adding confectioners' sugar and 4 tablespoons kirsch gradually. Spread generously over cherry filling. Add middle layer of cake and spread with remaining cherry filling and some of the whipped cream. Add remaining cake layer and frost with remaining whipped cream. Decorate with reserved whole cherries and chocolate curls.

Black Forest Cake (above)

easter

As the sun rises on Easter morning in the Southland, its light falls on diverse and time-honored Easter celebrations. The Greeks who settled in southern Florida . . . the French in Louisiana . . . the Mexicans in Texas . . . the Scots-Irish of Appalachia . . . every group in the melting pot which is America's South celebrates this holiest of Christian holidays in its own unique way.

These traditional celebrations center around holiday foods, and we've included some of these foods on the menu for Easter (page 6). To help you celebrate this holiday in southern fashion, recipes for these and other delicious Easter foods are in the pages that follow.

These are the recipes for dishes *Southern Living* homemakers serve with pride to both family members and holiday guests. You'll delight in recipes for southern-style meats . . . mouth-watering, spring-fresh vegetables . . . and beautiful cakes and candies that are so much a part of everyone's Easter celebration.

Every recipe in these pages is the home-tested favorite of a woman who has carefully chosen ingredients to create a dish which is uniquely her own. Almond Tea, for example, with its soft aroma and sharp flavor, brings a hint of the Mediterranean to American homes. This is just one of the exciting recipes awaiting your attention in these pages, compiled to make your Easter celebration especially meaningful and memorable.

It's Easter, and the long, dark days of winter are officially over. Not only is Easter one of the holiest days in the Christian faith, it is also the signal that spring is here once again. Both for its religious significance and as a herald of warmer days, Easter is one of the most joyous holidays of the year. And it's one of the most exciting, too.

Remember the thrill of Easter when you were a child? The whole family rose early. You eagerly searched for your Easter basket filled with brightly colored eggs. You sometimes attended Easter sunrise service. Then there was the walk through the park or along the streets, seeing friends you hadn't seen for months, with everyone in new finery. Even today, we retain the charming custom of the Easter parade.

Easter is also a time when families gather together. For many families, it's

entertaining

FOR EASTER

the first time together since the Christmas holidays. With so much excitement in the air, thoughtful homemakers want to plan an exciting meal that is certain to be enjoyed by everyone. The menu you'll find in the beginning of this book for Easter focuses on two traditional Easter foods — eggs and lamb.

The recipe for Leg of Lamb with Buttered Mushrooms and Peas recalls the custom of serving the paschal lamb — the Easter lamb — a custom heavily symbolic for Christians everywhere. The serving of lamb at Easter was introduced into the Southland by Greeks who settled along the western and southern coasts of Florida. Here — along sponge-rich Gulf waters — they built a way of life very much like the one they had left on the shores of the Mediterranean. One tradition they continued in the New World was that of the paschal lamb. Imaginative southern homemakers adapted that custom to suit the tastes of their own families — with delicious results, as you'll find when you try the menu recipe.

With this dish, offer your family and guests Greek Easter Soup with Egg Sauce . . . Curried Egg Canape . . . and other foods which have become favorites with southern families. And here's a nice bonus for you: these dishes provide a delicious way to use up all those Easter eggs!

Once you have explored the recipes on our southern-style holiday menu, continue farther. In the pages that follow, you'll find a mouth-watering collection of favorite recipes for Easter foods served in thousands of southern homes from Maryland to Texas.

Many of these foods are the products of generations-old traditions. For instance, just as lamb is the traditional Easter meat in parts of Florida, so ham is featured prominently in tidewater Maryland. Here, in times past, Easter was the signal for a most unusual neighborhood competition. Families would vie to see which could produce the most delicious stuffed ham. Every family had its own carefully kept secret describing the perfect way to cure and prepare ham. The most important part of this preparation, Marylanders claimed, was the stuffing. The fine art of stuffing ham disappears north of the Mason-Dixon line, but in Maryland this art was developed to a fine peak. The best stuffings were a careful blend of herbs, spices, vegetable seasonings, hot liquid, and a bread base — usually corn bread. The ham was scored and stuffing packed into each hole. Or it was boned and the cavity filled with savory stuffing. Then the carefully stuffed ham was put into a medium oven. Throughout the evening before Easter, the house filled with the tantalizing aroma of baked ham. By Easter morning, the ham was cooked.

After church services on Easter Sunday, groups moved in progression from home to home, leisurely sampling the mouth-watering ham-and-stuffing concoctions awaiting their critical pleasure. As the day drew to a close, the group proclaimed one ham better than all others — the champion ham until next year when the fun and competition began once again.

From this tradition came a wide range of taste-tempting recipes — not just for ham but for side dishes that would complement the savory main dish being enjoyed. Some of these recipes are included in the pages that follow — waiting to give your family and guests as much pleasure on this Easter as they have other families on Easters past.

Once you have discovered the wonderful foods in this section, your thoughts may turn toward creating your own new Easter traditions. Why not try your hand at making an Easter bunny cake — an eye-pleasing and taste-tempting treat sure to be a hit with family and friends alike. This cake would make a delightful centerpiece for your holiday dinner — as would a lamb cake, a cake baked and decorated just like an Easter egg, or the delightful Easter basket cake described in the pages that follow.

Also in these pages, you'll find recipes to help you carry out a traditional — and fun-filled — Easter egg hunt. Not only are there cake recipes but recipes for old-fashioned, decorated Easter eggs . . . chocolate eggs . . . and that long-time southern favorite, spun sugar. Think how much your children and their friends would enjoy searching for these delicious eggs. Hide eggs around the house and yard. As your small guests arrive, give each one a basket. After everyone is there, let the hunt begin. The child who gets the most eggs wins a prize, perhaps an elaborately decorated, hollow egg with a gay scene inside.

With so many party ideas and recipes in this section, you're certain to have an Easter day that everyone will remember with pleasure for a long time to come.

STRAWBERRY PUNCH

2 1-lb. packages frozen
   strawberries,
   thawed

2 6-oz. cans frozen
   grapefruit juice
2 qt. ginger ale

Crush the strawberries and place in a punch bowl. Reconstitute the grapefruit juice and pour over the strawberries. Add ice. Add the ginger ale and serve. 25 servings.

Mrs. Mary Epps, Selma, Alabama

PINK FIZZ

2 qt. cherry soda
2 16-oz. bottles cola
   beverage

1 qt. cream soda
1 pt. vanilla ice cream

Chill the cherry soda, cola beverage and cream soda. Pour beverages into a punch bowl and add large scoops of ice cream. 32 punch cups.

Mrs. Earl Knight, Birmingham, Alabama

TEAHOUSE PUNCH

1/2 c. tea leaves
2 bunches fresh mint
Sugar
2 1-qt. 2-oz. cans pineapple
   juice
2 c. orange juice

2 c. lemon juice
2 c. grapefruit juice
2 sm. jars maraschino
   cherries
1 qt. ginger ale
1 qt. club soda

Teahouse Punch (above)

Pour 4 cups water into a saucepan and bring to a boil. Remove from heat and add tea. Cover and steep for 4 minutes. Stir and strain into a container holding 3 quarts cold water. Place the mint and 1/4 cup sugar in a large mixing bowl and crush with a wooden spoon. Stir in the fruit juices. Add the tea and sugar to taste and mix well. Strain and add the cherries. Pour over an ice ring in a punch bowl and add the ginger ale and club soda slowly. 70 servings.

ALMOND TEA

2 c. sugar	2 c. strong tea
3 pt. water	1 tsp. almond flavoring
Grated rind of 1/2 lemon	1 tsp. vanilla
Juice of 3 lemons	

Combine the sugar, 2 pints water and lemon rind in a saucepan and boil for 5 minutes. Add remaining ingredients and bring to a boil. Remove from heat and serve. 18 servings.

Mrs. R. M. Brady, Lexington, Kentucky

CURRIED EGG CANAPE

1 tbsp. mayonnaise	2 hard-cooked eggs, finely
1/4 tsp. salt	chopped
1/4 tsp. curry powder	Buttered bread slices

Mix the mayonnaise, salt, curry powder and eggs in a bowl. Cut the bread in desired small shapes and spread with butter. Spread with egg mixture. Garnish with carrot wedges, olive slices, pimento wedges and green pepper wedges.

Mrs. Ray Martin, Huntsville, Alabama

DEVILED EGGS DELUXE

6 hard-cooked eggs	1/4 tsp. salt
2 tsp. prepared mustard	Dash of pepper
1 1/2 tsp. Worcestershire	1/4 c. mayonnaise
sauce	1 6 1/2-oz. can grated tuna
2 tsp. lemon juice	Dash of curry powder

Cut the eggs in half lengthwise and remove yolks. Mash the egg yolks in a bowl. Add the mustard, Worcestershire sauce, lemon juice, salt, pepper and mayonnaise and mix well. Stir in the tuna and curry powder. Place in egg whites. One-half cup sour cream may be substituted for mayonnaise.

Ernestine Scott, Bedford, Kentucky

Easter Antipasto (below)

EASTER ANTIPASTO

8 artichokes	1/4 c. mayonnaise
1 1/2 tsp. salt	Yellow food coloring
2 8-oz. packages cream	12 hard-cooked eggs, chilled
cheese, softened	32 pimento-stuffed olives,
1/2 tsp. seasoned salt	halved

Wash the artichokes and cut off stems at base. Remove small bottom leaves. Trim tips of leaves and cut off about 1 inch from artichoke top. Reserve all leaves from top. Stand artichokes upright in deep saucepan large enough to hold snugly and place reserved leaves around artichokes. Add the salt and 2 to 3 inches boiling water and cover. Simmer for 35 to 45 minutes or until artichokes may be pierced easily with fork. Remove artichokes and turn upside down to drain. Drain the leaves. Spread leaves of bottoms of artichokes apart gently and remove choke from center with spoon. Chill artichokes and leaves. Place bottom halves of artichokes in center of serving plates. Blend the cream cheese, seasoned salt and mayonnaise in a bowl and add enough yellow food coloring for bright yellow color. Place in a pastry bag with a star tip and half fill centers of artichokes with cheese mixture. Pipe additional cheese mixture around edges of artichokes. Place 1 egg in center of each artichoke and pipe remaining cheese mixture onto egg as desired to resemble decorated Easter Egg. Garnish each artichoke with olive half. Cut remaining eggs in eighths lengthwise. Surround each artichoke with cooked leaves, sliced eggs and remaining olives. Chill. 8 servings.

CREAMED CHICKEN PUREE

1 3-lb. chicken, disjointed	2 stalks celery with leaves
2 or 3 sprigs of parsley	1 onion, sliced
1 sprig of thyme	1 sm. carrot, diced

1 slice lemon peel	1/2 c. rice
6 peppercorns	2 egg yolks
Salt to taste	1 c. heavy cream

Place the chicken in a large saucepan and add 6 cups boiling water, parsley, thyme, celery, onion, carrot, lemon peel, peppercorns and salt. Simmer until chicken is tender. Remove chicken from broth and cool. Remove chicken from bones. Dice part of the chicken breast for garnish and grind remaining chicken. Strain the broth and add enough water to make 1 quart liquid, if needed. Pour into a saucepan. Add the rice and cook until tender. Add the ground chicken and simmer for 30 minutes. Puree in a blender and return to saucepan. Place over low heat. Beat the egg yolks in a bowl and stir in the cream. Stir in small amount of the hot soup. Stir back into the soup and cook, stirring, for 3 minutes. Do not boil. Add salt and ladle into soup bowls. Garnish each serving with small amount of the reserved chicken.

Mrs. George Garrett, Hagerstown, Maryland

GREEK EASTER SOUP WITH EGG SAUCE

1 1/2 lb. lamb	Salt and pepper to taste
6 tbsp. butter	3 eggs
2 lge. green onions	6 tbsp. lemon juice
4 sprigs of dillweed	

Cut the lamb in large pieces and place in a saucepan. Add 1 quart water and bring to a boil. Reduce heat and simmer for 25 minutes, removing the scum as it accumulates. Remove the lamb and chop fine. Melt the butter in a skillet and add the lamb. Chop the scallions and dillweed fine and add to lamb. Cook for 15 minutes, stirring occasionally. Strain the broth and add enough water to make 2 quarts liquid. Season with salt and pepper and add the lamb mixture. Simmer for about 1 hour. Remove from heat and cool slightly. Place the eggs, lemon juice, and 1 tablespoon water in a large bowl and beat well. Add the hot soup slowly, stirring vigorously, and serve immediately.

Mrs. Bert Powell, Staunton, Virginia

EASTER FRUITS

1 lge. can pineapple chunks	1 can mandarin oranges
1 lge. can peach halves	2 or 3 bananas, sliced
1 lge. can pear halves	Brown sugar
1 lge. can purple plums	Chopped pecans to taste

Drain the canned fruits well and mix. Place layer of canned fruits in a casserole and add layer of bananas. Repeat layers until casserole is full, then cover top with sugar. Add the pecans. Bake in 350-degree oven for 30 minutes. 18-20 servings.

Mrs. C. D. Huston, Greenwood, Mississippi

FROSTED HONEYDEW SALAD

1 pkg. red raspberry
  gelatin
1 1/2 c. hot water
2 c. red raspberries

1 honeydew melon
1 8-oz. package cream
  cheese
1 tbsp. cream

Dissolve the gelatin in hot water in a bowl and chill until thickened. Stir in the raspberries. Pare the honeydew melon. Cut a slice from 1 end and remove seeds. Drain well. Place melon upright in a bowl and fill with gelatin mixture. Replace cut slice and secure with toothpicks. Chill until gelatin is firm. Whip the cream cheese with cream until fluffy and spread on melon.

Cornelia Miller, Murfreesboro, Tennessee

FRESH GRAPEFRUIT MARINE SALAD

3 grapefruit, chilled
3/4 lb. cooked crab meat
  or shrimp
1/2 c. sliced celery

1/4 c. sliced pimento olives
1 c. mayonnaise
1 tsp. Worcestershire sauce
Snipped fresh parsley

Cut the grapefruit in half crosswise and cut around each section with a sharp knife to loosen from membrane. Remove sections with a spoon carefully and drain well. Scrape remaining membrane from shells, leaving shells clean and intact. Drain the crab meat. Combine the grapefruit sections, crab meat, celery and olives and place in the grapefruit shells. Chill until very cold. Combine the mayonnaise and Worcestershire and spoon over each serving. Garnish with parsley and serve on bed of crushed ice, if desired. 6 servings.

Fresh Grapefruit Marine Salad (above)

CARROT-RAISIN SALAD WITH SOUR CREAM

4 lge. carrots, scraped
1/2 c. seedless raisins
1/2 c. chopped pecans
3/4 tsp. salt

Pepper to taste
2 tsp. grated lemon peel
1 tbsp. lemon juice
1 c. sour cream

Place the carrots in ice water for 1 hour. Drain and grate coarsely into a bowl. Add the raisins, pecans, salt, pepper, lemon peel and juice and mix lightly. Add the sour cream and toss.

Mrs. H. L. Crumly, Birmingham, Alabama

MR. McGREGOR'S SALAD BOWL

1 pkg. lime gelatin
1 1/2 tsp. garlic salt
3/4 c. hot water
Dash of pepper
3/4 c. sour cream
1/4 c. mayonnaise
1 tbsp. vinegar
1 2-oz. can anchovies, minced

1 9-oz. package frozen
   artichoke hearts
1 grapefruit, sectioned
1 c. sliced tomatoes
1/2 c. sliced olives
1/4 c. chopped green onions
3 qt. salad greens

Dissolve the gelatin and garlic salt in hot water in a bowl and add the pepper, sour cream, mayonnaise, vinegar and anchovies. Beat with rotary beater until blended and pour into a shallow pan. Chill until firm and cut into 1-inch squares. Cook the artichoke hearts according to package directions and drain. Cut each artichoke in half and chill. Combine the grapefruit, tomatoes, olives and green onions in a large bowl. Tear the salad greens into small pieces and toss with olive mixture. Chill. Add the artichokes and toss lightly. Arrange anchovy squares on top.

French Dressing

1 c. water
1 c. sugar
2 cloves of garlic, minced
1 c. catsup
2/3 c. vinegar
1 c. salad oil

1 tbsp. prepared mustard
1 tsp. salt
1/2 tsp. pepper
1/2 tsp. paprika
2 or 3 drops of hot sauce
1 tsp. Worcestershire sauce

Mix the water, sugar and garlic in a saucepan and cook until slightly thickened. Cool. Pour into a quart jar and add remaining ingredients. Cover and shake well. Serve with salad. French dressing may be refrigerated for several days for improved flavor.

Betty Pate, Clinton, Arkansas

LAMB WITH MUSHROOMS AND PEAS

4 tbsp. lemon juice	12 lge. mushroom caps
1 clove of garlic, crushed	1/4 c. butter
1 leg of lamb	1/4 c. water
Salt	1 10-oz. package frozen
Pepper	green peas
Ground thyme	Pimento strips

Combine 3 tablespoons lemon juice and garlic and brush on the lamb. Sprinkle lamb with salt, pepper and thyme to taste and place on rack in a shallow roasting pan. Roast in 325-degree oven for 35 minutes per pound or to 175 degrees on meat thermometer for medium doneness. Place on a platter. Saute the mushroom caps in butter and remaining lemon juice in a skillet until tender. Place on platter with lamb and keep warm. Add the water, 1/4 teaspoon salt, dash of pepper and dash of thyme to remaining butter in the skillet and bring to a boil. Add the peas and cover. Cook until peas are tender. Spoon peas over mushrooms and garnish with pimento. Two cups fresh green peas may be substituted for frozen peas.

Mrs. R. Shirley, Greensboro, North Carolina

LAMB RACK WITH ORANGE-FILLED AVOCADO HALVES

1 7-bone rack or loin of	2 oranges
lamb	2 avocados
Salt and pepper to taste	Lemon juice

Season the lamb with salt and pepper and place, fat side up, in a shallow roasting pan. Bake at 325 degrees to desired degree of doneness. Peel and section oranges. Cut avocados in half and remove seeds. Sprinkle with lemon juice. Fill centers of avocados with orange sections and place around lamb on serving platter. Serve with vinaigrette sauce.

Photograph for this recipe on page 62.

CHICKEN CROQUETTES

1 1/2 c. chopped cooked	1 tsp. salt
chicken	2 tbsp. water
2 tbsp. finely chopped onion	1 egg, slightly beaten
3/4 c. thick white sauce	1/2 c. finely chopped almonds
1/8 tsp. pepper	1 1/4 c. cracker crumbs

Combine the chicken, onion, white sauce and seasonings and shape into croquettes, using 1 rounded tablespoon for each. Mix the water and egg. Combine the almonds and cracker crumbs. Roll croquettes in crumb mixture. Dip into egg mixture, then roll in crumb mixture again. Let set for 10 minutes. Fry in deep fat at 375 degrees for 2 minutes. 4 servings.

Mrs. John Swain, Columbus, Mississippi

CREAMED CHICKEN IN TIMBALES

2 tbsp. butter or margarine	2 c. diced cooked chicken
2 tbsp. flour	2 hard-boiled eggs,
1/2 c. broth	chopped
1 1/2 c. cream of mushroom	Salt and pepper to taste
soup	

Melt the butter in a heavy skillet. Add the flour and stir until smooth. Add the broth and cook, stirring, until thick. Add the mushroom soup and blend thoroughly. Stir in the chicken, eggs, salt and pepper and heat through.

Timbale Cases

2 eggs, separated	Salad oil
1 c. water	1 1/2 c. flour

Beat the egg yolks in a bowl until lemon colored. Add the water, 1 tablespoon oil and flour and beat until smooth. Fold in stiffly beaten egg whites. Heat a timbale iron in oil to 365 degrees. Drain iron and wipe off excess fat. Dip iron in batter, being sure that batter adheres to outside iron only. Fry until medium brown. Remove from iron and place on absorbent paper. Serve the creamed chicken in Timbale Cases.

Mrs. B. F. Pierson, Little Rock, Arkansas

CHICKEN KIEV

4 med. chicken breasts	1 stick butter, chilled
Salt to taste	Flour
1/2 c. chopped green onion	2 eggs, well beaten
1/2 c. chopped parsley	1 c. fine cracker meal

Cut the chicken breasts in half lengthwise and remove skin and bone. Place chicken between 2 pieces of plastic wrap. Pound with a wooden mallet until 1/4 inch thick, then remove plastic wrap. Sprinkle chicken with salt, onion and parsley. Cut butter into 8 sticks and place 1 stick near end of each cutlet. Roll as for jelly roll, tucking in sides of chicken, and press to seal well. Dredge with flour and dip in eggs. Roll in cracker meal and chill at least 1 hour. Fry in deep fat at 340 degrees for about 15 minutes or until golden brown and drain on paper toweling.

Sauterne Sauce

6 tbsp. butter	2 sprigs of parsley, chopped
6 tbsp. flour	Garlic powder to taste
2 c. chicken broth	Worcestershire sauce to taste
1 1/2 c. dry sauterne	Horseradish to taste

Melt the butter in a saucepan and blend in flour. Cook over low heat until flour is brown. Add the chicken broth and cook until thick, stirring constantly. Add remaining ingredients and simmer for 30 minutes, stirring occasionally. Strain and serve with chicken. Sauce may be refrigerated for 1 week.

Mrs. Janet Tracy, Tampa, Florida

Easter Beef in an Egg Shell (below)

EASTER BEEF IN AN EGG SHELL

1 4 to 5-lb. beef	Butter
eye-of-round roast	Sifted flour
1 tbsp. prepared mustard	3 eggs
1 tbsp. soy sauce	1/3 c. white wine
Salt	Pepper to taste

Place the roast on a large sheet of foil. Mix the mustard and soy sauce and spread on the roast. Fold sides of foil over roast, making double fold, then fold ends upward and double back. Place in a shallow baking pan. Roast at 300 degrees for 3 hours, then chill. Open foil. Drain the roast and reserve liquid. Place the roast in a shallow baking pan and pat dry with paper towels. Pour 3/4 cup water into a saucepan and add 1/4 teaspoon salt and 6 tablespoons butter. Bring to boiling point. Add 3/4 cup flour all at once and stir over moderate heat until mixture forms a ball and follows spoon. Remove from heat and cool slightly. Beat in the eggs, one at a time, and cool. Spread over the roast, covering top, sides and ends, and decorate top as desired. Place on low shelf of oven. Bake at 425 degrees for about 30 minutes or until browned. Remove fat from reserved liquid and add enough butter, if needed, to make 2 tablespoons fat. Melt in a saucepan and blend in 2 tablespoons flour. Mix the wine with enough reserved liquid to make 1 cup liquid, adding water if needed. Stir into butter mixture in saucepan and simmer until thickened. Add salt to taste and pepper and serve with the roast. 8 servings.

VEAL PALERMO

1/4 c. flour	1/2 tsp. salt
1 c. grated Parmesan cheese	Dash of pepper

6 veal steaks	1 green pepper, thinly sliced
1 egg, beaten	1/2 c. barbecue sauce
Oil	1 8-oz. can tomato sauce
1 lge. onion, thinly sliced	Dash of garlic salt

Combine the flour, 1/2 cup cheese, salt and pepper. Dip the veal in egg, then in seasoned flour. Brown in small amount of oil in a skillet and place in a shallow baking dish. Top with onion and green pepper. Combine remaining ingredients and pour over onion mixture. Sprinkle with remaining cheese. Bake at 325 degrees for 35 minutes. 6 servings.

Pearl Scott, Gainesville, Florida

VEAL ROLLS SMITANE

1 1/2 c. fine bread crumbs	1/8 tsp. basil
2 tbsp. grated onion	2 tbsp. melted butter
1/4 tsp. salt	2 tbsp. snipped parsley
1/8 tsp. pepper	6 thin veal cutlets
1/8 tsp. poultry seasoning	6 thin slices boiled ham
1/8 tsp. chervil	1 c. chicken broth
1/8 tsp. tarragon	1 c. sour cream

Place the bread crumbs, onion, seasonings, spices, butter and parsley in a bowl and toss lightly. Cover each veal cutlet with 1 slice ham and top with crumb mixture, leaving a narrow border around edge. Roll as for jelly roll and tie with string. Brown in small amount of fat in a skillet over medium heat. Add the chicken broth and cover. Simmer for about 30 minutes. Remove rolls to a serving platter and remove strings. Add sour cream to drippings in the skillet and blend well. Pour over rolls. 6 servings.

Mrs. William J. Bryan, Shreveport, Louisiana

CABBAGE WITH SOUR CREAM

2 lb. red cabbage, shredded	1 tsp. caraway seed
1 c. sour cream	Salt and pepper to taste

Cook the cabbage in 1/4 cup boiling, salted water for 10 to 15 minutes or until tender. Stir in the sour cream, caraway seed and seasonings and heat through. 2 servings.

Mary Beth Stine, Chattanooga, Tennessee

CURRIED CABBAGE

1/2 to 1 tsp. curry powder.	1/2 med. cabbage, shredded
1/2 c. water	

Mix the curry powder and water in a saucepan and add the cabbage. Bring to a boil and reduce heat. Cover tightly and simmer for 10 minutes or until cabbage is tender.

Mrs. Tanner Jackson, Philadelphia, Mississippi

CARROTS WITH HERBS

2 bunches sm. carrots	1/3 tbsp. salt
2 tbsp. butter	2 tbsp. heavy cream
1/4 tsp. sugar	1 tbsp. chopped tarragon
1/2 tsp. monosodium glutamate	1/8 tsp. cracked pepper
2 lettuce leaves	Chopped fresh mint
2 tbsp. chopped parsley	to taste (opt.)

Cut the carrots in thin slices. Melt the butter in a skillet and add the sugar and monosodium glutamate. Add the carrots. Dip the lettuce leaves in water and place over carrots. Cover the skillet. Cook over low heat for 20 minutes, then remove lettuce leaves. Add remaining ingredients and mix well.

Mrs. Edward Gonyenbach, Manor, Texas

SCALLOPED EGGPLANT

1 eggplant	1 c. dry bread crumbs
1 egg, beaten	1 sm. onion, diced
1/2 c. milk	1/2 c. diced celery
2 tbsp. melted butter or	Buttered bread crumbs
margarine	Grated cheese

Cook the eggplant in boiling, salted water for 8 minutes. Drain and mash. Add the egg, milk, butter and dry bread crumbs and mix. Cook the onion and celery in small amount of water in a saucepan until tender, then drain. Stir into eggplant mixture and place in a baking dish. Cover with buttered crumbs and cheese. Bake at 325 degrees for 30 minutes.

Mrs. Oscar Erke, Fort Smith, Arkansas

LENTIL CASSEROLE

1 lb. lentils	1/8 lb. butter or margarine
2 tbsp. chopped onion	4 tbsp. flour
2 tbsp. chopped green	Light cream
pepper	1 tsp. seasoned salt
2 or 3 stalks celery,	1/2 tsp. salt
chopped	1 sm. can tomato sauce

Place the lentils in a saucepan and cover with water. Soak for several hours or overnight. Bring to a boil and cook until tender. Drain and reserve liquid. Saute the onion, green pepper and celery in butter in a saucepan until tender and add flour. Add enough cream to reserved liquid to make 3 cups liquid. Stir into onion mixture and cook until thickened, stirring constantly. Add the seasonings, tomato sauce and lentils and pour into a 2-quart casserole. Bake at 350 degrees for 1 hour, stirring occasionally and adding water as needed. 8 servings.

Margaret Tisdale, Memphis, Tennessee

Spinach Florentine (below)

SPINACH FLORENTINE

2 lb. fresh spinach	6 lge. eggs
1/2 tsp. sugar	Hollandaise Sauce
3/4 tsp. salt	Grated Parmesan cheese (opt.)
1/4 tsp. pepper	

Preheat oven to 350 degrees. Wash the spinach and drain. Place in a saucepan and cover. Do not add water. Cook for 8 minutes or until spinach is wilted and tender. Add the sugar, salt and pepper and mix well. Run a knife through the spinach 2 or 3 times and place the spinach in 6 greased individual casseroles. Break an egg over the top of each casserole and sprinkle with additional salt and pepper to taste. Bake for 20 minutes or until eggs are set. Serve with Hollandaise Sauce and Parmesan cheese.

Hollandaise Sauce

3/4 c. butter or margarine	Dash of salt
2 1/2 tsp. lemon juice	Dash of cayenne pepper
3 lge. egg yolks, well beaten	

Place 1/4 cup butter in top of a double boiler and add the lemon juice and egg yolks. Place over hot, not boiling, water and cook, beating constantly with a wire whisk or beater, until butter is melted. Add 1/4 cup butter and cook, beating constantly, until mixture begins to thicken. Add remaining butter and cook until sauce is consistency of mayonnaise, beating constantly. Remove from water immediately and add the salt and cayenne pepper.

CURRIED CREAMED EGGS

1/3 c. butter or margarine	1/2 tsp. curry powder
1/2 c. chopped celery	3 c. milk
1/4 c. chopped green pepper	6 hard-cooked eggs, sliced
1/3 c. flour	2 tbsp. chopped pimento
1 1/2 tsp. salt	

Melt the butter in a saucepan. Add the celery and green pepper and cook over low heat until tender. Blend in the flour, salt and curry powder. Add the milk and cook, stirring constantly, until thickened. Add eggs and pimento and heat through. Serve on hot, buttered toast points, toasted English muffin halves or biscuits. 4-6 servings.

Mrs. Jay Fowler, Ft. Myers, Florida

DEVILED EGG BAKE

6 hard-cooked eggs, halved	1 5-oz. can shrimp
1/4 c. mayonnaise or salad	1 can frozen shrimp soup,
dressing	thawed
2 tsp. prepared mustard	1/2 c. milk
1/4 tsp. salt	4 c. cooked rice

Remove the egg yolks and place in a bowl. Mash well. Blend in the mayonnaise, mustard and salt and place in egg whites. Drain the shrimp, devein and rinse. Place in a saucepan and stir in the soup and milk. Cook over low heat, stirring frequently, until bubbly. Spoon rice into a 6-cup shallow baking dish and arrange eggs on rice. Pour shrimp mixture over top. Bake at 350 degrees for 15 minutes or until heated through. Garnish with parsley. 6 servings.

Mrs. Henry Vachon, Charlotte, North Carolina

CROISSANTS

1 1/2 c. butter	1/4 c. sugar
Sifted flour	1 tsp. salt
2 pkg. dry yeast	1 egg, beaten
1/4 c. warm water	1 egg yolk
Milk	

Cream the butter in a bowl and stir in 1/3 cup flour. Roll between 2 sheets of waxed paper to 12 x 6-inch rectangle and chill thoroughly. Dissolve the yeast in warm water. Scald 1 cup milk. Stir in the sugar and salt and cool to lukewarm. Add the yeast and egg and mix well. Add 3 3/4 cups flour or enough to make soft dough and mix well. Knead on lightly floured surface for about 5 minutes or until smooth and glossy and roll out to 25 x 7-inch rectangle. Place chilled butter mixture on half the dough and fold over remaining dough, sealing edges well. Roll on lightly floured surface to 20 x 12-inch rectangle. Fold 1/3 of the rectangle over center third and fold remaining third over. Chill. Repeat rolling and folding twice and cut crosswise in fourths. Chill for 30 minutes. Roll out 1 portion on lightly floured surface to 21 x 8-inch rectangle, and cut into 12 wedges so that each has a 4-inch base and is 7 inches long. Roll each wedge from wide end toward point. Place 3 inches apart on ungreased baking sheets, point down, and curve ends to form crescents. Repeat with remaining dough. Cover and let rise for 1 hour or until doubled in bulk. Beat the egg yolk with 1 tablespoon milk and brush on tops of rolls. Bake at 375 degrees 12 to 15 minutes or until lightly browned.

Mrs. Carol Scott, Hickory Flats, Mississippi

EASTER BREAD

1 c. scalded milk	2 eggs, well beaten
1/2 c. sugar	5 c. (about) sifted flour
1 tsp. salt	9 uncooked sm. eggs in shell
1/4 c. corn oil	1 egg white, beaten
1/4 c. warm water	1 c. light corn syrup (opt.)
1 pkg. dry yeast	

Mix the milk, sugar, salt and corn oil and cool to lukewarm. Pour the water into a warm mixing bowl. Sprinkle with yeast and stir until dissolved. Add the milk mixture, beaten eggs and 3 cups flour and beat until smooth. Mix in enough remaining flour gradually to make soft dough. Turn out onto floured board or cloth and knead until smooth and elastic. Place in a greased bowl and turn to grease top. Cover. Let rise in a warm place, free from draft, for about 1 hour or until doubled in bulk. Punch down. Shape half the dough into 9 small rolls and place on a greased cookie sheet. Cover and let rest for 15 minutes. Make 1 1/2-inch cut in center of each roll and place 1 egg in each. Cover with a cloth. Shape remaining dough into a large round loaf and place on a greased cookie sheet. Cover. Let rolls and loaf rise for 30 to 45 minutes or until doubled in bulk. Brush with egg white. Bake at 375 degrees for 20 minutes for rolls and 30 minutes for loaf. Bring corn syrup to a boil in a saucepan and brush on hot bread. Let set for several minutes before serving. Each half dough may be shaped into three 22-inch ropes, braided, shaped into circle and ends pinched together to fasten. Let rise and bake as directed for rolls.

Easter Bread (above)

HOT CROSS BUNS

2 pkg. dry yeast	3 1/2 to 4 c. sifted
1/2 c. warm water	all-purpose flour
1/3 c. scalded milk	1 tsp. cinnamon
1/2 c. salad oil or melted	3 eggs, beaten
shortening	2/3 c. currants
1/3 c. sugar	1 egg white, slightly beaten
3/4 tsp. salt	3/4 c. sifted confectioners' sugar

Dissolve the yeast in water. Mix the milk, oil, sugar and salt in a bowl and cool to lukewarm. Combine 1 cup flour and cinnamon and stir into milk mixture. Add the eggs and beat well. Stir in the yeast and currants. Add enough remaining flour to make soft dough and beat well. Cover with a cloth and let rise in warm place until doubled in bulk. Punch down and turn out on lightly floured surface. Cover and let rest for 10 minutes. Roll out 1/2 inch thick and cut with biscuit cutter. Place 1 1/2 inches apart on greased baking sheet. Cover and let rise until doubled in bulk. Cut cross in top of each bun and brush with egg white. Bake at 375 degrees for 15 minutes and cool slightly. Mix the confectioners' sugar with remaining egg white and place in a pastry tube. Pipe in shape of cross on each bun. 2 dozen.

Mrs. Doddie Griffiths, Palm Beach, Florida

CHANTILLY EASTER ANGEL CAKE

2 c. whipping cream	1 pt. fresh strawberries,
1 c. crushed pineapple,	sliced and sweetened
drained	1/2 tsp. vanilla
12 marshmallows,	1 angel food cake
diced	1 c. toasted coconut

Whip the cream in a bowl until stiff and fold in pineapple, marshmallows, strawberries and vanilla. Cut the cake in half crosswise and spread 1/3 of the strawberry mixture on bottom layer. Top with remaining cake layer and spread remaining strawberry mixture over top and side of cake. Sprinkle top and side with coconut and chill for several hours.

Mrs. Flo A. Hurt, Paint Rock, Texas

NAPOLEON CREMES

1 c. butter	1 3 3/4-oz. package instant
1/4 c. sugar	vanilla pudding mix
1/4 c. cocoa	4 1/2 c. confectioners'
1 1/2 tsp. vanilla	sugar
1 egg, slightly beaten	1 3-oz. package cream
2 c. finely crushed graham	cheese
crackers	1/8 tsp. salt
1 c. flaked coconut	2 oz. unsweetened chocolate,
5 tbsp. milk	melted and cooled

Combine 1/2 cup butter, sugar, cocoa and 1 teaspoon vanilla in a saucepan and cook over low heat until butter is melted. Stir in egg slowly and cook for 3 minutes, stirring constantly. Blend in crumbs and coconut and press into a greased 9 x 13-inch pan. Cream remaining butter in a bowl and stir in 3 table-spoons milk, pudding mix and 2 cups confectioners' sugar. Beat until fluffy. Spread over crust and chill until firm. Beat the cream cheese in a bowl until fluffy. Add remaining confectioners' sugar alternately with remaining milk and beat until smooth. Add the salt, remaining vanilla and chocolate and beat until well mixed. Spread over pudding mixture and chill. Cut into 2 x 3/4-inch bars. 80 bars.

Mrs. Allen Wallace, Greenville, South Carolina

ICE CREAM PARFAIT MOLD

2 1-lb. packages frozen strawberries, thawed	2 pt. vanilla ice cream
Milk	1 c. whipping cream, whipped
2 3-oz. packages strawberry gelatin	Green shredded coconut (opt.)

Drain the strawberries and reserve syrup. Add enough milk to reserved syrup to make 1 3/4 cups liquid. Pour into a saucepan and bring to a boil. Add the gelatin and stir until dissolved. Cut each pint ice cream into 8 pieces. Add to gelatin mixture and stir until ice cream is melted and blended. Chill until partially set. Fold in the strawberries and pour into an oiled melon mold. Chill until firm. Unmold and decorate Easter egg-fashion with whipped cream and coconut. Cut in slices to serve. 8-10 servings.

Ice Cream Parfait Mold (above)

ANGELICA

1 1/2 c. sugar	**1/8 tsp. salt**
1/2 c. water	**1 tsp. vanilla**
2 egg whites	**1 1/2 pt. whipping cream**

Combine the sugar and water in a saucepan and bring to a boil. Cook until syrup spins a thread. Beat the egg whites in a bowl until stiff. Add the syrup slowly, beating constantly, then cool. Add vanilla. Beat the cream until stiff and fold into egg white mixture. Pour into a mold and freeze. Place alternate layers of Angelica and desired fruit or syrup in parfait glasses and garnish with candied violets.

Mrs. L. V. Meskill, Fairfield, Alabama

FROZEN LEMON MOUSSE

Vanilla wafer crumbs	**1/2 c. lemon juice**
6 eggs, separated	**1/2 pt. cream, whipped**
1 1/4 c. sugar	

Cover bottom of 9-inch square baking dish with crumbs. Beat the egg whites until stiff, adding sugar gradually. Add the egg yolks, one at a time, beating well after each addition. Add the lemon juice and beat well. Fold in whipped cream and turn into crumb-lined dish. Cover top with crumbs and freeze. 12 servings.

Mrs. Virgil Hanson, Hamilton, Mississippi

EASTER BUNNIES

1 pkg. cake mix	**Red food coloring**
2 tbsp. shortening	**Coconut**
1 1/2 c. confectioners' sugar	**Cherry morsels**
1/2 tsp. vanilla	**Cinnamon**

Prepare the cake mix according to package directions. Place in paper liners in muffin pans and bake according to package directions. Cool. Cream the shortening and sugar in a bowl. Add the vanilla and enough food coloring to tint pink. Frost each cake and dip in coconut. Make eyes with cherry morsels and mouth with cinnamon. Cut ears from pink construction paper. Make whiskers from chenille pipestems and fasten to cakes.

Mrs. Dorothy Shanks, Mobile, Alabama

CHERRY EASTER EGGS

1 lb. confectioners' sugar	**2 drops of vanilla**
1/4 lb. butter	**1 8-oz. jar maraschino**
1 c. shredded coconut	**cherries**
1 c. chopped walnuts	**2 lge. milk chocolate bars**

Mix the sugar and butter in a bowl until mixture resembles cornmeal. Add the coconut, walnuts and vanilla and mix. Drain and chop the cherries and stir into the coconut mixture. Shape into 6 eggs and refrigerate until cold. Melt chocolate bars in a double boiler, then spread on eggs with a knife. Refrigerate for at least 24 hours.

Mrs. Marty Varley, Birmingham, Alabama

NO-COOK FONDANT

1/3 c. margarine	1/2 tsp. salt
1/3 c. light corn syrup	1 lb. confectioners' sugar,
1 tsp. vanilla	sifted

Blend the margarine, corn syrup, vanilla and salt in a large mixing bowl. Add the confectioners' sugar all at once and mix with a spoon, then knead with hands. Turn out onto a board and continue kneading until mixture is well blended and smooth. Store in refrigerator and shape as desired. 1 1/3 pounds.

Spun Sugar

1/3 c. water	1 c. sugar
1/4 c. light corn syrup	

Combine all ingredients in a small saucepan and bring to a boil over medium heat, stirring constantly. Boil, without stirring, to hard-crack stage or to 310 degrees on a candy thermometer. Remove from heat. Grease the handles of 2 wooden spoons and tape spoons to table top 12 inches apart with handles extending over edge of table. Spread newspapers on floor under spoon handles to cover an area several feet wide. Dip a fork, preferably with 6 prongs, into syrup and shake rapidly back and forth over greased handles, dipping fork and shaking until desired amount of spun sugar accumulates. Remove strands from handles carefully. Repeat until all syrup mixture is used, working quickly. Shape spun sugar as desired. Use the same day, since spun sugar melts upon standing at room temperature.

No-Cook Fondant (above)

State Fair Cranberry-Apple-Nut Pie (page 100)

fourth of july

Summertime . . . hot, lazy days with high temperatures and even higher humidity. These are the days which seem literally to melt into each other.

Yet even in the midst of that blur, there are some days that stand out sharply. The Fourth of July is one, with its firecrackers lighting up a dark summer sky . . . parades . . . flags . . . and the inevitable cookout or picnic.

The Fourth of July is a holiday anxiously awaited in villages and cities of the South. School children anticipate the excitement of the annual parade while older members of the family are looking forward to this year's family reunion.

Family reunions are the highlight of summers in the Southland. From hundreds of miles around, all branches of the family gather at a central picnic ground, church-yard, or family-owned farm. Each group proudly displays its tastiest dishes for the reunited family to view and, best of all, to savor.

The menu on page 7 contains dishes typical of what you and your family would find at such a southern family reunion — Anchovy Stuffed Eggs, Green Tomato Pickles, Western Spit-Roasted Ham, and, of course, Hearty Potato Salad. Why not begin now to explore the recipes for these and other dishes you'll find on the following pages — recipes certain to make your Fourth of July memorable!

85

Fourth of July — a lovely, lazy time when you can plan a wonderful family reunion. If you were lucky enough to enjoy family reunions as a child, surely you have a rich potpourri of memories — the ever-building excitement . . . the thrill of seeing uncles, aunts, and cousins you hadn't seen for a year or more . . . the new babies . . . the competition to see who had grown the most. And the marvelous old ice cream freezer! Cranking it was never work; it was a delightful privilege the children fought over.

Family reunion time down South is a very special event. For months before, letters move across the region, inviting this or that branch of the family to come home once again. After some debate, the meeting place is decided upon. Whatever place is selected, it is certain to have plenty of playing room for children, good cooking facilities, broad picnic tables for the many deli-

entertaining
FOR FOURTH OF JULY

cious foods, and perhaps even an old-fashioned swimming hole!

Beginning early on the morning of the reunion, cars and pickup trucks arrive at the chosen place. Proud women bring out great baskets heaped with food. The men select a place for the barbecue pit or cookfire. Children eye one another shyly until someone proposes a game all can share in. As the voices mingle and the day's heat rises, the reunion begins.

Shouldn't your children have the opportunity to experience all the wonderment of a family reunion at least once in their lives? And how marvelous for you to recapture the spirit of family togetherness once again! This Fourth of July could be your time to renew this great American custom.

And what better way to renew it than at a great meal featuring the foods you'll find in this section! You'll discover recipes, not just for the dishes suggested on the Fourth of July menu (page 7), but for many other typically southern dishes just right to serve at family get-togethers.

If you're organizing the reunion as a picnic or an all-day outing, be sure to plan well in advance. If you're counting on obtaining needed firewood at the site, don't. It's best to bring your own. Similarly, if you plan to buy corn, watermelon, or any other locally grown picnic foods, be sure to check in advance with local produce growers. Let them know what your anticipated needs will be. Then, if they can't supply you, you'll have plenty of time to shop. Do bring blankets, flashlights, a good first aid kit, and mosquito repellent. These items might not be needed, but it is best to be prepared for any contingency.

To reduce your preparation and clean-up time — and to leave you free to visit with your family — try using paper supplies. Don't confine yourself to the usual paper napkins, but enjoy the brightly colored tablecloths, cups, and plates. Another nice-to-have item is foil-wrapped, damp face cloths — a must to clean sticky faces and hands.

What about packing the foods? Most areas large enough to accommodate a family reunion will have a stove that can be used to heat casseroles, rolls, and meats that are to be served hot. Cold food should be wrapped in waxed paper or foil — never in a damp towel — and refrigerated immediately after preparation. Chill the food thoroughly — overnight chilling is best. Pack these chilled foods last and try to be sure they are eaten first. This care will reduce the possibility of meats or salads turning bad in the heat.

Let each family group bring enough food for itself. Then put all the dishes out and let each person choose for himself what he would like. Sure, you'll probably get five bowls of potato salad. But each salad will be subtly different from the other — and what a wonderful taste treat for everyone!

Don't forget the ice cream freezer. Southerners know that no family reunion is complete without the ice cream freezer. Let the children take turns cranking it — making ice cream is not work to a child, it's a glorious adventure!

For eye-pleasing tables, cover them with red-and-white checkered tablecloths. Plastic ones for the children and cloth for the adults will cut down on your cleaning-up time. Many camping goods stores sell plastic clamps which will hold down tablecloths against even the strongest winds.

And do plan table decorations that shout with Fourth of July colors. Take pieces of celery and dip the ends in paprika. Put the opposite ends in a glass of water (to be sure the celery stays crisp), and serve. Jellied cranberry sauce cut into the shape of stars . . . pimento strips and strips of tomato aspic . . . radish roses . . . strawberries, raspberries, and blueberries massed in a huge glass bowl . . . striped peppermint candies . . . watermelon balls mixed with bright plums . . . foods covering a wide range of bright colors and mouthwatering tastes.

With all the delicious and filling food you're bound to have, some activity will be welcome. Croquet and pitching horseshoes are old-fashioned activities as enjoyable today as they were long ago. And everyone loves to play softball. Don't forget the games you played as a child . . . potato sack races . . . treasure hunts . . . hide-and-seek . . . hare and hounds. Your children will delight in these time-honored games just as you once did.

By the end of this memorable Fourth of July, you'll be heading home, sunburned, full of delicious home-cooked food, and with warm memories of family love and togetherness that are sure to last until next year's Fourth of July family reunion. Why not begin to plan your wonderful day right now, by browsing through the tried-and-proven recipes in the following pages.

Hawaiian Punch (below)

HAWAIIAN PUNCH

3 c. unsweetened pineapple juice	3/4 c. lemon juice
1 1/2 c. unsweetened orange juice	2 tbsp. liquid sweetener
	2 qt. carbonated water, chilled

Combine the juices and sweetener and chill. Add carbonated water just before serving and garnish with lemon slices or pineapple spears. Serve immediately. 3 1/4 quarts.

REGATTA DAY PUNCH

1 c. sugar	1 8-oz. bottle lemon juice
4 c. water	1 7-oz. can crushed pineapple
1 46-oz. can orange drink	1 4-oz. bottle maraschino cherries, chopped
1 46-oz. can pineapple juice	Quart bottles of ginger ale

Mix the sugar and water in a saucepan and bring to a boil, stirring until sugar is dissolved. Remove from heat and cool. Add remaining ingredients except ginger ale and mix well. Pour 1 quart ginger ale into 1/2-gallon milk carton and fill carton with pineapple mixture. Repeat until all pineapple mixture is used.

Freeze. Remove from freezer 1 hour and 30 minutes before serving to allow partial thawing. Break up frozen punch to form slush. 40 servings.

Mrs. Jim Chandler, Riviera, Texas

CRANBERRY DELIGHT

Lime sherbet   Cranberry juice

Place 1 scoop sherbet in 6-ounce glass; pour cranberry juice over sherbet, filling glass. Serve immediately.

Mrs. Bobby Sichling, Harvey, Illinois

WATERMELON SHELL PUNCH

1 watermelon
1 6-oz. can frozen orange
  juice
1 6-oz. can frozen lemonade

1 6-oz. can frozen limeade
4 c. cold water
1 lge. bottle ginger ale,
  chilled

Remove top third of watermelon and scoop out all but 1 inch of melon. Trim top of shell with a scalloped edge. Combine the orange juice, lemonade, limeade and water and pour over ice cubes in melon shell. Garnish with slices of lemons, oranges and small cubes of watermelon. Add ginger ale just before serving. 12-15 servings.

Mrs. Jeanne Guernsey, Blytheville AFB, Arkansas

CLARET LEMONADE

1 jigger grenadine syrup   Chilled soda water
Juice of 1 lemon

Place the syrup and lemon juice in a tall glass. Place 3 or 4 ice cubes in the glass and fill to the top with soda water.

Mrs. Fulton White, Amarillo, Texas

SANGRIA

2 jiggers unsweetened grape   Dash of lemon juice
  juice   1 tsp. sugar syrup
2 jiggers pineapple juice   Soda water

Fill a highball glass half full with crushed ice. Pour grape juice, pineapple juice, lemon juice and sugar syrup over the ice and mix thoroughly. Fill the glass with soda water.

Pauline Metts, Augusta, Georgia

Hot Olive Dip (below)

HOT OLIVE DIP

2 c. heavy cream	1 clove of garlic, finely chopped
4 to 8 flat anchovy fillets	1/3 c. chopped stuffed
1/4 c. butter or margarine	olives

Pour the cream into a saucepan and bring to a boil. Reduce heat and simmer, stirring frequently, for about 20 minutes or until cream is reduced to 1 cup. Rinse the anchovy fillets, drain and chop fine. Melt the butter in a 1-quart heat-proof casserole over low heat. Stir in the anchovies, garlic, olives and cream and bring to a simmer, stirring constantly. Do not boil. Place over candle warmer and serve with Italian bread sticks, celery, carrot, cucumber or green pepper strips, radishes, scallions, cherry tomatoes, mushroom halves or cauliflowerets.

ANCHOVY-STUFFED EGGS

6 hard-cooked eggs	2 tbsp. finely chopped
1/4 c. mayonnaise	anchovy fillets
Dash of pepper	

Cut the eggs in half lengthwise and remove egg yolks. Mash the egg yolks and blend in mayonnaise and pepper. Stir in anchovies. Fill egg whites with yolk mixture and chill. Garnish with diced pimento and parsley. 6 servings.

Mrs. Patricia Jeffries, Alexandria, Louisiana

FRENCH-DEVILED EGGS

1 doz. hard-cooked eggs	1 tsp. chopped parsley
Mayonnaise	Salt and pepper to taste
1 c. chopped cooked shrimp	Garlic powder to taste

Cut the eggs in half lengthwise. Remove egg yolks and mash. Add enough mayonnaise to moisten. Add the shrimp and parsley. Add salt, pepper and garlic powder and mix well. Fill egg whites with shrimp mixture. Garnish with small sprigs of parsley and paprika.

Mrs. Larry Hyland, Miami, Florida

CHEESE BALL

1 8-oz. package cream cheese	1 lb. Velveeta cheese, grated
4 sm. glasses Cheddar process cheese spread	2 sm. onions, grated
	1 tbsp. Worcestershire sauce
2 sm. glasses blue cheese spread	1/2 c. walnuts, crushed (opt.)

Have all cheeses at room temperature. Mix cheeses, onions and Worcestershire sauce. Roll into 2 balls and roll balls in walnuts. Chill thoroughly and serve with crackers. 20 servings.

Mrs. Frank Harris, Tuscaloosa, Alabama

FIRECRACKER CHEESE JALAPENOS

1 pkg. Cheddar cheese, grated	1 sm. jar pimento strips
Mayonnaise	1 jar jalapeno peppers

Mix the cheese with enough mayonnaise to moisten. Drain the pimentos and stir into the cheese mixture. Remove seeds and stems from jalapeno peppers and stuff with cheese mixture. 10 servings.

Mrs. Bill McCraw, Raymondville, Texas

GREEN TOMATO PICKLES

48 sm. green tomatoes	2 qt. water
6 cloves of garlic	1 qt. vinegar
6 stalks celery	1 c. salt
6 sm. green peppers	Dill to taste

Pack the tomatoes into sterilized jars. Add 1 clove of garlic, 1 stalk celery and 1 green pepper, cut into fourths, to each jar. Mix the water, vinegar, salt and dill in a saucepan and bring to a boil. Cook for 5 minutes, then pour over tomatoes in jars. Seal at once. Store for 4 to 6 weeks before serving. 6 quarts.

Mrs. Nancy Odom, Fairfield, Alabama

SEAFOOD SALAD MEDLEY

1 7-oz. can chunk tuna, drained	1 tbsp. capers
1 c. cooked cleaned shrimp	Green Mayonnaise
1 tbsp. lemon juice	Salt and pepper to taste
2 hard-cooked eggs, sliced	Lettuce
1/2 c. sliced celery	Cucumber slices
2 tbsp. minced green onion	Paprika

Combine the tuna and shrimp and sprinkle with lemon juice. Add the eggs, celery, onion and capers and chill. Add 1/2 cup Green Mayonnaise, salt and pepper and toss lightly. Serve in lettuce cups and garnish with cucumber slices and paprika. Serve remaining Green Mayonnaise with salad.

Green Mayonnaise

2 eggs	2 cloves of garlic
Juice of 1 lemon	3/4 tsp. dry mustard
1 tsp. vinegar	1 1/4 tsp. salt
3 green onions, sliced	1 pt. salad oil
1 tsp. parsley	

Place all ingredients except oil in a blender and blend well. Add oil gradually and blend until thick.

Lulu Smith, Sand Springs, Oklahoma

TUNA-CORN CHIP SALAD

1 6 1/2-oz. can tuna, drained	1/2 c. chopped celery
1/2 c. crushed corn chips	2 tbsp. chopped onion
1/2 c. chopped green pepper	1/8 tsp. pepper
	Mayonnaise

Combine first 6 ingredients in a bowl and stir in enough mayonnaise to moisten. Refrigerate until chilled. 4 servings.

Mrs. Walter Cox, Panama City, Florida

ANTIPASTO SALAD

1/2 sm. head cauliflower	1 3-oz. jar pitted green olives
2 carrots, cut in 2-in. strips	3/4 c. wine vinegar
2 stalks celery, cut in 1-in. pieces	1/2 c. olive oil
1 green pepper, cut in 2-in. strips	2 tbsp. sugar
1 4-oz. jar pimento	1 tsp. salt
	1/2 tsp. dried oregano
	1/4 tsp. pepper
	1/4 c. water

Separate the cauliflower into flowerets and slice. Place in a skillet and add the carrots, celery and green pepper. Drain the pimento and olives and cut the pimento in strips. Add pimento, olives and remaining ingredients to cauliflower mixture and bring to a boil, stirring occasionally. Reduce heat and cover. Simmer for 5 minutes, then cool. Refrigerate for 24 hours and drain well before serving. 6-8 servings.

Mrs. William A. Chater, Charlotte, North Carolina

FRUIT SALAD IN WATERMELON BOWL

1 10-lb. watermelon	2 tbsp. lemon juice
1 head lettuce, shredded	1 env. low-calorie Italian
3 or 4 bananas, sliced	salad dressing mix
1 pt. fresh blueberries	2/3 c. orange juice
1 grapefruit, sectioned	

Split the watermelon in half horizontally and chill one half. Slice a piece from the bottom of remaining half to prevent watermelon from rolling. Scoop out center into balls or cut in cubes and remove seeds. Place watermelon balls in a bowl. Cover and chill. Remove remaining pulp from same half of the watermelon down to white rind, leaving about 1 inch of the red portion in bottom. Cut top edge with a sharp knife to resemble handles of a bowl. Place watermelon bowl on a platter and place lettuce in bottom of watermelon. Top with rows of watermelon balls, banana slices and blueberries. Place the grapefruit sections on top in shape of a flower and garnish with a fresh strawberry and mint leaves, if desired. Pour 1/4 cup water and lemon juice into a jar and add the salad dressing mix. Cover and shake until thoroughly blended. Add the orange juice and shake well. Pour part of the dressing over fruits and serve remaining dressing with salad. 6-8 servings.

Fruit Salad in Watermelon Bowl (above)

HEARTY POTATO SALAD

6 med. potatoes	Salt and pepper to taste
2 eggs	3/4 c. salad dressing
1/2 med. onion, chopped	1 tbsp. prepared mustard
1 tbsp. chopped green pepper	1 tbsp. sweet pickle
1 stalk celery, chopped	vinegar
4 med. sweet pickles, chopped	2 slices fried bacon,
6 stuffed olives, sliced	crumbled

Cook the potatoes in jackets in enough water to cover for 20 minutes or until done but still firm. Boil the eggs in water for 10 minutes and cool. Peel the potatoes and eggs and chop in 1-inch cubes. Add the onion, green pepper, celery, pickles and olives and sprinkle with salt and pepper. Combine the salad dressing, mustard and pickle vinegar. Add to potato mixture and mix well. Place the bacon on top and chill before serving.

Photograph for this recipe on page 96.

TOMATO L'OIGNON

3 lge. Bermuda onions	1 1/2 tbsp. salt
1 2-oz. can pimentos	1/2 c. water
3 tbsp. sugar	Ripe tomatoes
1/2 c. vinegar	Romaine or leaf lettuce
1 c. salad oil	

Grind the onions and pimentos in a food mill and place in a quart jar. Add the sugar, vinegar, salad oil, salt, and water and cover the jar. Shake well, then refrigerate for several hours to blend flavors. Peel and slice the tomatoes, allowing 3 slices per serving, and arrange overlapping slices on a bed of romaine. Cover with onion sauce.

Mrs. Pat Neal, Tallahassee, Florida

BALICHI

1 4 to 5-lb. eye of round	1/2 tsp. sweet basil
roast	3 tbsp. orange juice
3/4 c. salad oil	1 long link smoked sausage
1/4 c. tarragon vinegar	Salt and pepper to taste
1 clove of garlic, crushed	

Have the butcher cut 1 to 1 1/2-inch hole lengthwise through center of roast. Combine remaining ingredients except sausage, salt and pepper for marinade and pour several tablespoons marinade into cavity in roast. Fill cavity with sausage link and season the roast with salt and pepper. Place in a pan and pour remaining marinade over roast. Marinate for 12 to 24 hours. Drain, reserving marinade. Wrap the roast in foil and seal edges. Grill for 1 hour, then remove foil. Grill to desired doneness, basting occasionally with reserved marinade. 6 servings.

Mrs. Will McDonald, Mobile, Alabama

HAMBURGER PIE

1 lb. hamburger	1 8-oz. can tomato sauce
1 1/2 tsp. salt	2 tbsp. minced onion
1/4 tsp. pepper	1 c. grated mozzarella cheese
1 tsp. Worcestershire sauce	2 tbsp. chopped parsley
1 tsp. mustard	1/4 tsp. oregano
1 No. 2 can tomatoes, drained	

Combine the hamburger, salt, pepper, Worcestershire sauce and mustard and press against bottom and side of 9-inch pie plate. Spread tomatoes and tomato sauce over hamburger mixture and sprinkle with remaining ingredients. Bake at 375 degrees for 30 to 45 minutes. 4-6 servings.

Mrs. Claudia Smith, Waco, Texas

WESTERN SPIT-ROASTED HAM

3/4 c. cider vinegar	1/2 tsp. monosodium glutamate
3 orange slices, quartered	2 tsp. hot sauce
3 thin lemon slices	1/8 tsp. pepper
2 tbsp. Worcestershire sauce	1 tbsp. mixed pickling spice
1 tsp. salt	1 beef bouillon cube
2 tbsp. dark corn syrup	1/4 c. catsup
1 tsp. dried mint leaves	1/2 tsp. dried basil leaves
1/4 tsp. allspice	1/2 c. water
1 tsp. dry mustard	1 10 to 12-lb. whole
1/8 tsp. paprika	fresh ham

Combine the vinegar with orange and lemon slices in blender container. Cover and blend for 2 minutes. Pour into a medium saucepan and add remaining ingredients except ham, mixing well. Bring to a boil, stirring constantly. Reduce heat and simmer for 10 minutes. Skin, bone and roll the ham. Tie with string. Secure ham on spit and insert meat thermometer into ham. Adjust spit 8 inches from prepared coal and place foil drip pan under ham to catch drippings. Roast ham for 4 hours and 30 minutes or until temperature registers 185 degrees, basting frequently with sauce. Let stand for 15 minutes before carving.

Mary Martha Brown, Savannah, Georgia

GLAZED BACON ROAST ON THE SPIT

1 2-lb. roll Canadian bacon	1/4 c. prepared mustard
1/2 c. whole cranberry sauce	2 tbsp. honey

Secure the bacon on a spit. Mix remaining ingredients and spread over bacon. Place foil drip pan under bacon to catch drippings. Roast over hot coals for 50 to 55 minutes, basting frequently with drippings. 6-8 servings.

Mrs. Lisa Street, Tuscumbia, Alabama

CHARCOAL-BROILED T-BONE STEAKS

6 lge. T-bone steaks
1/2 c. melted butter
2 tbsp. Worcestershire sauce

2 tsp. garlic powder
1 tsp. salt

Have steaks at room temperature. Combine remaining ingredients. Place the steaks on a grill 5 to 6 inches above coals and grill for 5 minutes. Turn and baste with butter mixture. Repeat turning and basting until desired doneness is reached. Serve steaks with remaining butter mixture. 6 servings.

Mrs. Jack James, Bowling Green, Kentucky

SPIT-ROASTED LEG OF MUTTON

1/2 c. lemon juice
1/4 c. olive oil
1 lge. clove of garlic,
   crushed
1/2 tsp. pepper

1/2 tsp. thyme leaves
1/2 tsp. basil leaves
1 leg of mutton
Salt to taste

Combine the lemon juice, oil, garlic, pepper, thyme and basil in a large, shallow dish. Add the mutton and turn until coated with marinade. Refrigerate for several hours, turning mutton occasionally. Drain mutton and reserve marinade. Secure leg of mutton on rotisserie spit, balancing to rotate evenly, and sprinkle with salt. Cook for 25 to 30 minutes per pound or until meat thermometer registers 175 degrees for medium doneness, basting occasionally with reserved marinade. 6-8 servings.

Spit-Roasted Leg of Mutton (above); Hearty Potato Salad (page 94); Strawberry Pie (page 115)

Barbecued Game Hens with Spicy Stuffing (below)

BARBECUED GAME HENS WITH SPICY STUFFING

3 1/2 c. day-old bread crumbs	1/2 c. chopped celery
1/2 c. chopped sweet mixed pickles, drained	1/4 c. butter or margarine
1/2 c. diced dried figs	4 1-lb. frozen Rock Cornish game hens, thawed
1 egg, slightly beaten	2 tbsp. melted butter or margarine
1/4 tsp. salt	Barbecue sauce
1/8 tsp. poultry seasoning	Sweet mixed pickles

Mix the bread crumbs, chopped pickles, figs, egg, salt and poultry seasoning in a bowl. Saute celery in the butter in a saucepan for 1 minute. Add to the bread mixture and toss. Stuff in cavities of hens and truss. Arrange hens on spit of rotisserie. Cook for 1 hour or until tender and well browned, brushing occasionally with melted butter and barbecue sauce. Serve with sweet mixed pickles.

CRUSTY HERB-FRIED CHICKEN

1 3 to 3 1/2-lb. chicken	1/2 tsp. rosemary
1/2 tsp. thyme	1 tbsp. minced parsley
1/2 tsp. marjoram	1/2 tsp. salt
1 c. flour	1/4 tsp. pepper
3/4 c. oil	3/4 c. water

Cut the chicken in serving pieces. Sprinkle with thyme and marjoram and let stand for 30 minutes to 1 hour. Roll in flour and fry in hot oil in a frying pan until brown on both sides. Place in a baking pan and sprinkle with rosemary, parsley, salt and pepper. Pour water into frying pan and stir well. Pour liquid over chicken. Bake at 375 degrees for 40 to 45 minutes. 4-5 servings.

Mrs. Bob Fields, Columbia, South Carolina

DRUMSTICKS OVER THE FENCE

1/4 c. catsup	1/2 tsp. monosodium
2 to 3 tbsp. lemon juice	glutamate
2 tbsp. soy sauce	12 chicken drumsticks
1/4 c. salad oil	

Combine all ingredients except the drumsticks and mix well. Add drumsticks and stir to coat. Refrigerate overnight or let stand at room temperature for 2 hours, basting occasionally. Drain drumsticks and reserve marinade. Grill over low coals for about 25 minutes, basting with reserved marinade occasionally. Turn and grill for 20 minutes or until tender, basting occasionally with marinade. 6 servings.

Mrs. T. R. Stewart, Fort Benning, Georgia

BEEF FILLING ON FRENCH LOAVES

Cooked beef roast	Salt to taste
Chopped pickles	Mayonnaise
Chopped celery	Small French loaves

Grind the beef and stir in desired amounts of pickles and celery. Add salt and enough mayonnaise to moisten. Cut loaves in half and spread with beef mixture.

Mrs. Bill Lane, Athens, Georgia

MOZZARELLA CHEESE LOAF

1 sm. loaf unsliced Italian	Soft butter
or French bread	Anchovy fillets
Thinly sliced mozzarella cheese	Oregano to taste

Slice the bread not quite through at 1/2-inch intervals. Place cheese slices between the slices of bread and brush the loaf generously with butter. Place on a baking sheet and arrange thin strips of anchovy fillets on top. Sprinkle with oregano. Bake at 450 degrees for about 10 minutes or until the cheese is melted and the bread is golden.

Mrs. Stewart Biggs, Baltimore, Maryland

BUTTERMILK CORN BREAD

1 c. cornmeal	2 tbsp. sugar
1 c. sifted flour	1 egg
1 tsp. soda	1 c. buttermilk
4 tsp. baking powder	3 tbsp. melted shortening
1 tsp. salt	

Sift the dry ingredients together. Beat egg with buttermilk in a bowl. Add dry ingredients and mix well. Stir in the shortening and pour into a hot, greased 8 x 10-inch pan. Bake at 425 degrees for 30 minutes.

Mrs. E. Horman, Sr., Cocoa Beach, Florida

SEEDED WHITE BREAD

5 1/2 to 6 1/2 c. unsifted flour	1 1/2 c. water
3 tbsp. sugar	1/2 c. milk
2 tsp. salt	3 tbsp. margarine
1 pkg. dry yeast	1 egg white, beaten
	1 tbsp. poppy seed

Mix 2 cups flour, sugar, salt and yeast thoroughly in a large bowl. Combine the water, milk and margarine in a saucepan and place over low heat until liquids are warm. Margarine does not need to melt. Add to dry ingredients gradually and beat for 2 minutes with electric mixer at medium speed, scraping bowl occasionally. Add 3/4 cup flour and beat at high speed for 2 minutes, scraping bowl occasionally. Stir in enough remaining flour to make a soft dough. Turn out onto a lightly floured board and knead for 8 to 10 minutes or until smooth and elastic. Place in a greased bowl, turning to grease top, and cover. Let rise in a warm place, free from draft, for about 1 hour or until doubled in bulk. Punch down and turn out onto a lightly floured board. Cover and let rest for 15 minutes. Roll into a 16 x 9-inch rectangle, then roll as for jelly roll, starting from the 16-inch side. Pinch seam to seal and place in a greased 10-inch tube pan, sealed edge down. Seal ends together firmly and press dough down so that it fully covers bottom of pan. Cover and let rise in a warm place, free from draft, for about 1 hour or until doubled in bulk. Brush ring lightly with beaten egg white and sprinkle with poppy seed. Bake at 400 degrees for about 40 minutes or until done. Remove from pan and cool on a wire rack.

Seeded White Bread (above) Poppy Seed Braided Bread (page 165)

NEVER-FAIL CHOCOLATE CAKE

1 egg	1 tsp. vanilla
1/2 c. (scant) cocoa	1 tsp. soda
1/2 c. shortening	1/4 tsp. salt
1 1/2 c. flour	1 c. sugar
1/2 c. sour milk or	1/2 c. boiling water
buttermilk	

Place all ingredients in a bowl in order listed, then mix with electric mixer until smooth. Pour into a greased and floured 9 x 13-inch baking pan. Bake at 350 degrees for 35 to 40 minutes or until done.

Mrs. Nelson Barnes, Bryson City, North Carolina

STATE FAIR CRANBERRY-APPLE-NUT PIE

1 pkg. pie crust mix	1/2 c. sugar
3 med. apples	3 tbsp. flour
1 1-lb. can whole cranberry	1 tsp. cinnamon
sauce	1/2 tsp. nutmeg
1/2 c. chopped nuts	2 tbsp. melted butter or
1/2 c. seedless raisins	margarine

Prepare the pie crust mix according to package directions. Roll out 2/3 of the pastry to a 10-inch circle and place in a 9-inch pie pan. Remove cores from the apples and chop apples fine. Combine with remaining ingredients and pour into pastry-lined pan. Roll out remaining pastry and cut in 1/2-inch strips. Attach strips to rim of pastry. Press and twist strips across filling and press firmly. Fold excess pastry over strips and flute edge. Bake in 425-degree oven for 40 to 50 minutes or until filling is bubbly and crust is browned. Serve warm.

Photograph for this recipe on page 84.

HOMEMADE ICE CREAM IN CONES

5 eggs	1 lge. can evaporated milk, whipped
3 c. sugar	2 pt. half and half
1 tbsp. vanilla	Milk

Beat the eggs in a bowl until lemon colored. Add the sugar, 1 cup at a time, and beat well. Add the vanilla and evaporated milk. Add the half and half and pour into a 1-gallon ice cream freezer. Add enough milk to fill can 3/4 full and cover. Freeze with ice and salt according to ice cream freezer directions. Serve scoops of ice cream in cones.

Mrs. Shelby West, Nashville, Tennessee

CHILLED MELON BALLS

1/2 c. sugar	2 c. cantaloupe balls
1/2 c. grape juice	2 c. watermelon balls
4 tbsp. lemon juice	2 c. honeydew balls
1 c. water	

Combine the sugar, grape juice, lemon juice and water in a saucepan and bring to a boil. Cook for 1 minute. Cool and chill. Chill the melon balls. Arrange melon balls in serving cups and pour sugar mixture over balls. Garnish with maraschino cherries and mint leaves. 8 servings.

Mrs. Eva McKinley, Arkadelphia, Arkansas

FROZEN COUNTRY CHERRY CREAM WITH FRUIT SAUCE

1 8-oz. jar red maraschino cherries	1 3 1/2-oz. can flaked coconut
4 c. sour cream	1/2 c. red currant jelly
1 c. sugar	1/4 tsp. grated lemon peel
	2 tbsp. lemon juice

Drain the cherries and reserve syrup. Add enough water to reserved syrup to make 1/2 cup liquid. Chop the cherries. Combine 1/3 cup cherries with the sour cream, sugar and coconut and mix well. Pour into a 1-quart souffle dish and freeze until firm. Combine the cherry syrup mixture and jelly in a saucepan and stir over medium heat until jelly is melted. Add remaining cherries, lemon peel and juice and chill. Serve with the sour cream mixture. 8-10 servings.

Frozen Country Cherry Cream with Fruit Sauce (above)

Tomato Aspic Ring (page 108)
Italian-Barbecued Spareribs (page 110)

labor day

Labor Day comes while the southern summer's heat is still strong. Although other areas may consider Labor Day as a milestone to mark the end of summer, for Southerners the day is a holiday to rest from work and enjoy the summer activities.

One of the most popular traditions in the South is that of barbecuing or cooking out on Labor Day. Neighbors and friends are invited over to share in the holiday fun. One family may provide all the food, or the guests may each bring a dish. In any case, the foods are certain to be long-time southern favorites.

For the menu on page 7, *Southern Living* readers have contributed their favorite outdoor foods, foods like Gazebo Crab Dip, named for the old-time garden house . . . Family-Style Chateaubriand . . . Fresh Corn on the Cob . . . and other just-right-for-outdoors dishes.

The foods for this menu were chosen from the many recipes you'll find in the section that follows. Each recipe is the proud creation of a southern homemaker who cooks for her own pleasure and that of her family and friends. Every dish has passed the most critical of all tests: it has brought compliments to the woman who served it. Now these recipes are yours to cook . . . to serve . . . to bring you warm compliments at your Labor Day backyard party.

103

Outdoor entertaining is a long-time southern tradition. During the 1800's, entire families would enjoy leisurely visits at plantations, visits which went on for many months. Such visits led to many outdoor parties — barbecues, picnics, garden teas, and leisurely afternoon soirees under huge and ancient trees.

Now these months-long visits are a thing of the past. But the tradition of outdoor entertaining is still honored throughout the Southland. And of all outdoor parties, perhaps none is so beloved as the barbecue.

Barbecuing is a way of outdoor cooking that Southerners have enjoyed for generations. Every town — small or large — has its barbecue expert. When someone is planning an extra-special party, he calls in this expert. Early on the morning of the big party, the man and his helpers arrive. They dig the

entertaining
FOR LABOR DAY

pit, line it with stones, and begin their aromatic, smoky fires. Once the fire is ready for cooking, a grill is placed over it and the meat is set on that grill or over it on a spit.

Throughout the remainder of the morning and into the afternoon, the barbecuer patiently turns the meat, basting it with his own unique barbecue sauce. By later afternoon, as shadows begin to cross the pit, party guests hungrily gather closer, sensing as only Southerners can that the barbecue is nearly ready. At a signal, the long-patient guests are served — and the delicious food they enjoy is well worth waiting for.

These elaborate preparations were once the pleasure of only those who had time and money to spare. But today, with the advent of the backyard grill, barbecuing has spread out of the South to become a national pastime everyone can enjoy.

Labor Day, with its three-day weekend, is an ideal time for a barbecue party. And the menu you'll find on page 7 was designed especially to help you barbecue southern style. Every dish on this menu is the tried-and-proven favorite of a southern family. Recipes for these and other dishes are included in the section that follows, a section sure to give you many ideas for a delightful Labor Day barbecue.

Southern families know that barbecues are parties the whole family can enjoy — another good reason for having a barbecue party at Labor Day, when the family is back together after a summer of varied activities. Why not include your friends and neighbors in your party this year? Every family could contribute one dish — and you contribute the party setting.

The focal point of every barbecue is, of course, the meat dish. Whether your preference is for the elegant Chateaubriand featured on our menu or for one of the many other barbecue foods, your choice is endless. You may serve the all-American hamburgers and hot dogs . . . fish . . . seafood such as shrimp or lobster . . . barbecued spareribs . . . steak . . . ham . . . mixed grill . . . or poultry. If you are serving poultry, it should be cooked on a spit. A very plump chicken may be barbecued directly on the grill but all other poultry will become dry unless it is spitted and well basted while it cooks.

Almost as important as the meat are the foods you serve to accompany it. Breads are among the most beloved foods in American cuisine, and a barbecue is a great time to serve piping hot breads and rolls. Perhaps you'll make your own or add your own unique touch to bakery bread. Just be sure to have plenty — outdoor appetites make short work of hot bread!

Vegetables are another important dish for your barbecue. Corn on the cob — roastin' ears as they're called in the Southland — is a traditional favorite. You can cook corn in foil on top of your grill or boil it in the kitchen and bring it to your party table. Frozen vegetables can easily be cooked on your grill. Unwrap the packages and place the vegetables in a square of heavy-duty foil. Add seasonings to taste, seal tightly, and let the vegetables thaw at room temperature for three hours. Then pop them on your grill and serve directly from the foil package. Easy and good tasting! You'll need to allow about 30 to 40 minutes for nine- or ten-ounce packages of all vegetables except green beans, which take 50 minutes.

Be sure to have lots and lots of beverages for your thirsty guests. Iced tea — sweet and with a twist of lemon and a sprig of mint — is the usual barbecue drink in southern homes. Your family may prefer lemonade . . . punch . . . fruit juice . . . or perhaps coffee.

Plan your menu carefully, with an eye not just for serving complementary foods but for cooking times. A successful barbecue takes advance planning, and a most important part of that planning is scheduling cooking times. Start your fire early, and allow about 30 to 45 minutes from the time you light the fire until the time you start cooking. If you think you will need more charcoal, arrange it on the edge of the fire area: cold charcoal added to a hot fire slows down the cooking process.

When your barbecue is ready, keep the service simple. One of the best and easiest ways to serve is on paper plates. Have wicker liners available to prevent leaks, spills, and burned hands. Let each guest pick up his own plate and liner and move directly to the grill where the chef can serve him. Be sure to include plenty of paper napkins — they'll be needed!

With careful planning, the many delicious recipes you'll find in the pages that follow, and your own imagination, you're certain to have an unforgettable Labor Day barbecue!

GAZEBO CRAB DIP

1 8-oz. package cream cheese	1 tbsp. lemon juice
1 pkg. frozen crab meat, well drained	1 tbsp. horseradish Milk

Mix all ingredients, adding enough milk to moisten, and place in a casserole. Bake at 350 degrees until heated through. Serve with potato chips.

Mrs. Edith Browning, Clemson, South Carolina

LANAI DEVILED HAM DIP

1 c. sour cream	1 tbsp. minced green onion
1 4 1/2-oz. can deviled ham	Dash of pepper
1 tsp. prepared mustard	1/4 tsp. sugar
1/2 tsp. celery salt	

Combine all ingredients in a bowl and blend thoroughly. Chill and serve with assorted crackers, potato chips or vegetables. 1 1/2 cups.

Verna Jackson, Troy, Alabama

VEGETABLE DIP

1/2 c. mayonnaise	1/2 tsp. prepared mustard
1/2 tsp. curry powder	Salt and pepper to taste

Blend all ingredients in a bowl and serve with crisp vegetable sticks. 6 servings.

Mrs. Kenneth Brown, Opelika, Alabama

CHILLED GAZPACHO

5 ripe tomatoes	1 1/4 c. tomato juice
1 cucumber	3 tbsp. salad oil
1 green pepper, chopped	2 tbsp. vinegar
1 onion, chopped	1/4 tsp. paprika
1 tbsp. chopped parsley	Salt and pepper to taste
1 clove of garlic, crushed	

Peel and chop the tomatoes and cucumber. Combine the tomatoes, cucumber, green pepper, onion, parsley and garlic in a blender. Cover and blend until smooth. Stir in tomato juice, oil, vinegar, paprika, salt and pepper and chill thoroughly. Serve in individual chilled soup bowls and place an ice cube in each bowl. Serve with buttered croutons, crackers or cheese bread. 6-8 servings.

Mrs. William B. Dabney, Decatur, Texas

SUMMERTIME BORSCHT

1 c. finely chopped cooked beets	3 cans consomme 1/2 c. lemon juice
1 1/2 c. mixed beet stock and water	Sour cream Chopped chives or parsley

Combine the beets, beet stock and consomme in a saucepan and heat until well blended, stirring constantly. Remove from heat and add lemon juice. Chill thoroughly. Stir and pour into chilled bowls. Top with spoonfuls of sour cream sprinkled with chives. 8 servings.

Mrs. Jeanne P. Dabney, Albuquerque, New Mexico

RIPE OLIVE CHILI

2 1-lb. cans kidney beans	1 1-lb. can stewed tomatoes
1/2 lb. lean ground beef	1 8-oz. can tomato sauce
1 tbsp. cooking oil	1/2 tsp. salt

1 1 5/8-oz. package chili
    seasoning mix
	1 1/2 c. canned pitted ripe
	    olives

Drain and rinse the kidney beans. Cook the beef in oil in a skillet until lightly browned. Add the kidney beans, chili seasoning mix, tomatoes, tomato sauce and salt and simmer for 10 minutes. Drain the olives and add to beef mixture. Heat for several minutes longer. Serve as dip with tortillas. 6 servings.

Ripe Olive Chili (above)

TOMATO ASPIC RING

3 env. unflavored gelatin	1/3 c. lemon juice
5 c. tomato juice	1 tsp. onion juice
1/2 tsp. salt	1/4 tsp. hot sauce
1/8 tsp. sugar	

Mix the gelatin with 2 cups tomato juice in a saucepan. Place over moderate heat and stir constantly for 4 or 5 minutes or until gelatin is dissolved. Remove from heat. Stir in remaining tomato juice and remaining ingredients and pour into a 6-cup ring mold. Chill until firm. Unmold on a serving platter.

Shrimp Remoulade

1 c. creole or brown mustard	1/4 c. finely chopped celery
1 c. salad oil	1/4 c. finely chopped onion
1/2 c. catsup	1/4 c. finely chopped green
1/2 c. vinegar	pepper
1/2 tsp. hot sauce	2 lb. cooked cleaned shrimp

Combine the mustard, oil, catsup, vinegar, hot sauce, celery, onion and green pepper in a bowl and mix until blended. Add the shrimp and cover. Chill. Place in center of aspic ring just before serving.

Photograph for this recipe on page 102.

FISHERMAN'S TUNA SALAD

2 1/2 c. flaked tuna,	1/2 c. chopped celery
drained	Salt and pepper to taste
1 c. chopped nuts	Mayonnaise
2 hard-cooked eggs, chopped	Watercress
1/2 c. chopped sweet pickles	

Combine the tuna, nuts, eggs, pickles, celery, salt and pepper in a bowl and add enough mayonnaise to moisten. Serve on watercress. 6 servings.

Mrs. Evelyn Jones, Jackson, Tennessee

CABBAGE AND EGG SALAD

1 tsp. salt	1 tsp. grated onion
2 tsp. sugar	2 hard-cooked eggs, chopped
1/2 tsp. dry mustard	4 1/2 c. shredded cabbage, chilled
Dash of pepper	2 tbsp. chopped pimento (opt.)
1/4 c. evaporated milk	2 tbsp. chopped green
3 tbsp. vinegar	pepper (opt.)

Mix first 4 ingredients in a bowl. Add milk and stir until sugar is dissolved. Stir in the vinegar and onion and chill. Mix the eggs with cabbage, pimento and green pepper. Add the dressing and mix thoroughly. 4 servings.

Mrs. John S. Grooms, II, Dallas, Texas

HAWAIIAN FRUIT BOWL

1 No. 2 can pineapple chunks	1 can flaked coconut
1 sm. can seedless grapes	1 c. miniature marshmallows
1 sm. can mandarin oranges	1 pt. sour cream
1 sm. jar Royal Anne cherries	1/8 tsp. salt

Drain the pineapple, grapes, oranges and cherries and remove pits from cherries. Combine the fruits, coconut and marshmallows and mix well. Add the sour cream and salt and toss lightly. Refrigerate overnight.

Orlin R. Healy, Highlands, North Carolina

GOLDEN CREAM WALDORF

1 6-oz. package lemon gelatin	1/2 c. mayonnaise
1/4 tsp. salt	1 c. heavy cream, whipped
3 golden apples	1 c. finely chopped celery
Lemon juice	1/2 c. finely chopped walnuts

Dissolve the gelatin in 1 1/2 cups hot water in a bowl. Add 2 ice cubes and stir until melted. Stir in the salt until dissolved and chill until slightly thickened. Peel 2 apples, leaving small amount of peel for color. Core, dice and sprinkle with lemon juice. Cut remaining apple into thin slices and arrange slices, peel side down, around bottom of 8-cup ring mold. Sprinkle with lemon juice. Place in refrigerator to retain crispness. Blend the mayonnaise with gelatin and fold in the whipped cream. Stir in diced apples, celery and walnuts and spoon over apple slices. Chill until set. Unmold on salad greens and garnish with ripe olives.

Golden Cream Waldorf (above)

109

FAMILY-STYLE CHATEAUBRIAND

1 round steak, 2 in. thick	1 tbsp. prepared mustard
1 tsp. meat tenderizer	1 tbsp. Worcestershire sauce
1 c. tomato sauce	1 clove of garlic, minced
1/2 tsp. monosodium glutamate	1/4 c. chopped parsley
1 tbsp. sugar	1/2 to 1 c. Burgundy
1/4 c. butter or margarine	

Pierce steak with a fork and sprinkle on each side with meat tenderizer. Let set for 1 hour. Combine remaining ingredients except Burgundy in a saucepan and bring to a boil, stirring constantly. Reduce heat and simmer for 5 minutes. Cool and add Burgundy. Place grill 2 inches over coals. Slash fatty edges on steak and brush steak with sauce. Sear quickly on each side. Raise grill and continue to turn and baste steak until done. Slice diagonally.

Mrs. David Grant, Fort Worth, Texas

ITALIAN-BARBECUED SPARERIBS

3 1/2 lb. spareribs	2 onions, chopped
1 pkg. Italian salad dressing mix	2 tbsp. vinegar
2 tbsp. Worcestershire sauce	1 tsp. paprika
1 tbsp. salt	1 tsp. chili powder
3/4 c. catsup	1 c. water

Cut the spareribs in serving pieces. Prepare the salad dressing mix according to package directions and pour into a shallow pan. Marinate the ribs in the dressing for 4 hours or overnight in the refrigerator, then drain. Mix remaining ingredients and brush on the ribs. Cook over the coals, basting frequently, until done. May be wrapped in foil and cooked over coals, if desired. 8 servings.

Photograph for this recipe on page 102.

TERIYAKI PORK CHOPS

1 c. soy sauce	4 cloves of garlic, crushed
3/4 c. water	1 1-in. piece of gingerroot,
1/2 c. sweet vermouth	grated
1/2 c. honey	8 pork chops

Combine all ingredients except pork chops and mix well. Marinate chops in sauce in refrigerator overnight. Drain pork chops and reserve marinade. Broil pork chops over charcoal until done, basting frequently with reserved marinade. 4 servings.

Mrs. Bill Ellington,.Anniston, Alabama

MOCK KAHLUA ROAST

1 5-lb. boneless Boston butt	1/4 c. guava jelly
1/2 clove of garlic	2 tbsp. brown sugar
Salt to taste	

Rub Boston butt with garlic and sprinkle with salt. Wrap tightly in foil. Place on grill and cook over coals for 4 hours. Remove from foil. Mix the jelly with brown sugar and spread over Boston butt. Brown over coals for 10 to 15 minutes or until well glazed. 6 servings.

Mrs. Lewis Bailey, Jackson, Mississippi

GRILLED TROUT

1/4 c. French dressing	1/4 tsp. pepper
1 tbsp. lemon juice	6 dressed trout
1 tsp. salt	

Combine first 4 ingredients and brush each trout inside and out with sauce. Place on a grill over moderately hot coals and cook for 15 to 20 minutes. Turn and brush with sauce. Grill for 15 minutes longer or until trout flakes easily when tested with fork.

Mrs. Maurice Goolsby, Carthage, Texas

BARBECUED SOUTH AFRICAN ROCK LOBSTER-TAILS

6 frozen South African rock lobster-tails	1/2 c. melted butter
1/4 c. lemon juice	Salt to taste

Thaw the lobster-tails. Cut underside membrane around edge and remove. Grasp tail in both hands and bend backwards toward shell side to crack or insert skewers to keep tail flat. This will prevent curling. Combine the lemon juice, butter and salt. Grill the lobster-tails over hot coals for 5 minutes, flesh side down. Turn and brush with butter mixture. Grill, flesh side up, for 10 to 20 minutes or until lobster has lost its transparency and is opaque.

Barbecued South African Rock Lobster-Tails (above)

111

BARBECUED CHICKEN

3 sticks butter	1 bottle catsup
1 c. vinegar	Worcestershire sauce to taste
Lemon juice	1 tbsp. sugar
2 tbsp. salt	Red pepper to taste
8 chicken halves	

Combine 2 sticks butter, vinegar, 1 cup lemon juice, salt and 1 cup water in a saucepan and bring to a boil. Place chickens on grill and baste with sauce. Cook for 1 hour, turning and basting frequently. Combine remaining ingredients with remaining butter and juice of 2 lemons in a saucepan and heat until butter is melted. Cook chickens for 20 minutes longer, basting with catsup mixture frequently. 8 servings.

Emily Cooper, Daytona Beach, Florida

PICNIC-BAKED BEANS

1/2 c. chopped onions	1 sm. can evaporated milk
2 tbsp. butter	1 8-oz. can tomato sauce
1 1/2 tbsp. flour	1/2 c. grated American
2 or 3 tbsp. chili powder	process cheese
1/4 tsp. salt	1 1-lb. 12-oz. can baked
1/8 tsp. pepper	beans, drained

Saute the onions in butter in a saucepan until crisp-tender. Stir in the flour and seasonings. Stir in the evaporated milk and tomato sauce gradually and cook, stirring, until mixture boils for 1 minute. Add the cheese and beans and cook, stirring, until cheese is melted. Serve over frankfurter in roll with mustard and pickle relish, if desired. 4-6 servings.

Photographs for this recipe below and on page 37.

Picnic-Baked Beans (above)

BARBECUED CARROTS IN WINE

8 med. carrots, sliced
1/2 tsp. garlic salt
1/4 c. minced onion

1/2 c. consomme
1/4 c. sauterne

Place carrots on large sheet of heavy-duty aluminum foil and fold sides up to shape container. Sprinkle carrots with garlic salt and onion. Combine consomme and sauterne and pour over carrots. Seal foil lightly. Place on grill over hot coals and cook for about 20 minutes or until just tender, turning once.

Mrs. Ben Abbott, Wilmington, North Carolina

FRESH CORN ON THE COB

Ears of corn
Salt
Lemon juice

Butter
Pepper

Remove husks from corn and brush off silks. Drop in kettle in enough boiling water to cover and add 1 teaspoon salt and 1 teaspoon lemon juice for each quart water. Cover and cook for 5 to 8 minutes or until corn is tender. Remove from water and serve with butter, salt and pepper.

Mrs. Warren Knox, Greenwood, Mississippi

CHARCOALED ONIONS

6 med. onions, peeled
6 bouillon cubes

3 tsp. butter
Salt and pepper to taste

Scoop out small hole in top of each onion and fill with bouillon cube, butter, salt and pepper. Wrap separately and tightly in aluminum foil. Place on hot coals and cook for about 30 minutes, turning frequently. Unwrap and serve immediately. 6 servings.

Mavis Bush, Gadsden, Alabama

LEMON-NUT SQUARES

1 lb. butter or margarine
2 c. sugar
6 eggs
3 1/2 c. flour
1 tsp. baking powder

Pinch of salt
4 c. chopped pecans
1 15-oz. box raisins,
   floured
2 oz. lemon extract

Cream the butter and sugar in a large bowl. Add the eggs, one at a time, beating well after each addition. Sift dry ingredients together and stir into creamed mixture. Fold in remaining ingredients and pour into 2 greased and floured 13 x 9 x 2-inch loaf pans. Bake at 250 degrees for 2 hours and 30 minutes. Cool, then refrigerate for several hours before cutting. May be frozen.

Mrs. H. M. McKay, Baytown, Texas

BROWNIES

1/2 c. shortening	3/4 c. sifted cake flour
1 c. sugar	1/4 tsp. baking powder
2 eggs, beaten	1/2 tsp. salt
2 sq. unsweetened chocolate, melted	1 c. chopped walnuts or pecans

Cream the shortening in a bowl until smooth. Add the sugar, 2 tablespoons at a time, creaming well after each addition. Stir in the eggs and beat until smooth. Stir in the chocolate and mix until blended. Sift the flour, baking powder and salt together and add all at once to the creamed mixture. Add the walnuts and stir until blended. Turn into greased 8 x 8 x 2-inch baking pan. Bake at 350 degrees for 30 to 35 minutes or until done. Cut into bars or squares while warm. Cool and remove from pan. Store in covered container.

Mrs. Carl Funderburk, Monroe, North Carolina

STRAWBERRY BONANZA SHORTCAKE

4 c. prepared biscuit mix	2 pt. fresh strawberries, halved
Sugar	
1/2 c. melted butter or margarine	Orange or lemon marmalade
1 c. milk	1 pt. sour cream

Blend the biscuit mix with 1/4 cup sugar, butter and milk and knead gently 8 to 10 times on lightly floured surface. Pat out 1/3 of the dough in each of 3 greased 9-inch layer pans. Bake in 450-degree oven for 12 minutes or until lightly browned. Combine the strawberries and 2/3 cup sugar in a bowl and chill for 30 minutes. Stack biscuit layers, spreading each with thin layer of marmalade and 1/3 of the sour cream and strawberries.

Mrs. Ethel Tibbetts, Atlanta, Georgia

CHOCOLATE ICEBOX DESSERT

1/2 c. butter	1 tsp. vanilla
2 c. powdered sugar, sifted	1 c. chopped nuts
2 tbsp. cocoa	1 3/4 c. vanilla wafer crumbs
1/4 tsp. salt	
2 eggs, separated	

Cream the butter in a bowl. Add sugar, cocoa, salt and egg yolks and beat until mixed. Add the vanilla and nuts and mix well. Fold in stiffly beaten egg whites. Line a 9 x 9-inch pan with 1/2 of the vanilla wafer crumbs and pour in the cocoa mixture. Place remaining crumbs on top and garnish with maraschino cherries. Refrigerate overnight and serve with whipped cream, if desired. 6-8 servings.

Mrs. Margie R. Gilchrist, Borger, Texas

STRAWBERRY PIE

1 5/8 c. flour
1/2 c. butter or margarine
3 tbsp. cream or water
1 qt. strawberries

3 tbsp. sugar
1 tbsp. cornstarch
1 egg, beaten

Place the flour in a bowl and cut in the butter until of cornmeal consistency. Blend in the cream until dough clings together. Chill the dough thoroughly. Roll out half the dough on a floured surface and place in a 9-inch pie pan. Trim edge and prick bottom and side with a fork. Slice the strawberries lengthwise. Combine the sugar and cornstarch, then layer the strawberries and sugar mixture in the pie shell. Roll out the remaining dough and cut into strips with a pastry wheel. Arrange strips over top of pie in lattice fashion. Press strip around edge, sealing together. Brush with the egg. Bake at 400 degrees for 30 to 35 minutes or until pastry is brown. Cool before serving.

Photograph for this recipe on page 96.

SPICY CARAMEL PIE

1 1/4 c. vanilla wafer crumbs
3/4 tsp. cinnamon
1/4 tsp. nutmeg
1/4 c. melted margarine
2 c. cold milk

1 pkg. instant caramel-nut pudding
  mix
1/2 c. heavy cream
1 tbsp. sugar

Combine the vanilla wafer crumbs, 1/2 teaspoon cinnamon, nutmeg and margarine and mix until well blended. Press into an 8-inch pie plate. Bake at 350 degrees for 5 minutes, then cool. Pour the milk into a mixing bowl. Add the pudding mix and beat for about 1 minute or until smooth. Pour into the crust and chill for 30 minutes or until set. Beat the heavy cream with sugar and remaining cinnamon until stiff. Garnish the pie with part of the whipped cream and serve remaining whipped cream with pie.

Spicy Caramel Pie (above)

Frosted Pumpkin Doughnuts (page 130)

halloween

Witches . . . jack o'lanterns . . . black cats . . . pale clouds scurrying across a high-riding moon — it has to be Halloween. This holiday is beloved by both children and adults — perhaps because all of us enjoy a momentary escape into the wonderful world of make-believe. With its many costumes, fantastic decorations, and scary legends, Halloween does seem to be from another world. It's the perfect holiday for a party where you can let your imagination take you where it pleases!

On page 7, you'll find a marvelous Halloween party menu featuring dishes like Witches Cauldron . . . Diablo Eggs . . . Mephistopheles Dip . . . Black Sorcery Fondue . . . and other delightfully "other-world" foods. As exotic as these dishes sound, every one has been tried and proven by a southern homemaker. These are the foods women from Maryland to Florida serve, not only on Halloween but at parties and family meals throughout the year.

The recipes included in the pages that follow are just what you need to plan an extra-special Halloween party this year. In these pages, southern homemakers share with you their very best recipes for party-perfect foods. As you browse through this section, you too will be inspired to plan a party certain to take your Halloween guests into a marvelous, imaginative world full of delicious foods and fantasy.

117

Southern homemakers welcome the advent of Halloween as the signal for delightfully imaginative parties – and mouth-watering party foods! To set the atmosphere for your party, try writing the invitations on black masks with white ink. Mail them in plenty of time so that your guests will enjoy the added excitement of anticipation.

Decorate out-of-doors, too. If you've got a fence, top the posts with jack o'lanterns. Put grotesque masks outside your windows. Try painting a paper skeleton with luminescent paint, and hang him from a tree where he will move in the wind. To cast a truly ghost-like aura over your home, place bunches of blue and green Christmas lights near scarecrows, jack o'lanterns, and piles of autumn leaves.

There's always so much excitement over Halloween parties. These fun-filled

entertaining
FOR HALLOWEEN

events are always popular, especially among the younger set. Children of all ages adore dressing in costumes. And when they can dress in their spooky attire *and* go to a party, their joy knows no bounds! If you're giving a children's party, try to have at least three adults on hand for every 25 children. You'll need that many to cope with your excited young guests, to organize games, and to help hunt for lost overshoes and misplaced coats!

Very young children – under six years old – love parties but sometimes may hestitate to join in. To break the ice, have each child lie down on a big piece of paper while an adult traces around him. Children may color their "paper dolls" as they wish, and adults can help cut them out. At the end of the party, each child has something to take home (a good tactic when not everyone will win a prize!). Beanbag games are favorites with very young children. They love to try to hit wooden bottles, pins, or any designated target.

Party refreshments for the very young are best limited to finger foods – apple sections, small popcorn balls, pumpkin cookies, punch, and finger sandwiches. For very special party favors, give each child his own party mask.

Older children – six to about ten – love parties that feature traditional games. Bobbing for apples will be as popular with this group as it was when you were growing up. Remember the excitement of finding the apple that had a dime or a quarter stuck into it? You can capture that same excitement for your children. Just be sure to place a big piece of plastic under the bobbing bucket – water does get spilled in all the hilarity.

Try a Halloween version of "Pin the Tail on the Donkey" — "Pin the Tail on the Skeleton!" If you have an older child or adult who is willing to play the role, have a fortune-telling session. Children love it! By all means, include time for telling ghost stories. A crackling fire adds to the scary atmosphere, but if you don't have a fireplace, try building a centerpiece of leaves and cornstalks and surrounding it with blue and green Christmas lights. These lights make the centerpiece glow eerily and heighten the ghost-filled atmosphere. This age group will love traditional party fare.

A Halloween party for teenagers? Let your teenagers do most of the planning themselves — this is the "I'd-rather-do-it-myself" age group, remember? You might suggest a "Secret Ambition" party — each guest comes as his secret ambition and everyone tries to guess what that ambition is. Or a "Left Bank" party when everyone dresses as he imagines the Bohemian residents of Montmartre do. Games for this age group need to be creative . . . like a sculpturing contest. Each boy brings an uncut pumpkin. Boys and girls are paired and each couple is given a sharp knife, a candle, and plenty of newspapers to protect the floor. The object is to carve the most imaginative jack o'lantern. Prizes are awarded for the best and the worst sculpture. Then candles are placed inside the jack o'lanterns, and they are arranged around the party room. These glowing, grinning monsters build an atmosphere all their very own.

Dancing is a must at teenagers' parties and so is food. There's just one rule for these parties — whatever the refreshments are to be, be sure to have plenty on hand. Let your youthful host decide what he wants for party foods. You might suggest that he capitalize on the teenagers' independence and let them make their own goofy hamburgers — combinations of hamburger meat and condiments that are particular favorites of young guests.

But let's not limit Halloween parties to children and teenagers. After all, adults need to escape into the world of fantasy, too. Try a "Come as You Were" party — guests wear costumes to represent people they might like to have been in times past. Or perhaps a "Come as You Are" party — invitations are issued by telephone just an hour or so before the party, and guests must come dressed as they were when they received the invitation.

Party decorations should capitalize on the season, not only the Halloween holiday but the entire autumn spectacle. Brightly colored leaves wired in bunches . . . stalks of Indian corn . . . scarecrows . . . the variety of seasonal decorations is endless. And here again, you can use blue or green Christmas lights to cast an other-world glow over everything.

Yes, Halloween is your night to escape from the real world into a fantastic other land where strange things happen all the time . . . where anything is possible . . . where people we see every day turn into mysterious creatures with the help of a costume and a mask. With the aid of your own creative imagination, you can make your party the most fabulous, out-of-this-world event ever — just try it and see.

Butterscotch Punch (below)

BUTTERSCOTCH PUNCH

2 6-oz. packages butterscotch
   pieces
2 tbsp. butter or margarine
3 lge. cans evaporated milk

2 c. water
2 tsp. rum flavoring
Whipped cream
Nutmeg

Melt the butterscotch pieces and butter in a large saucepan over low heat. Stir in the evaporated milk and water gradually and cook over medium heat, stirring, until well mixed and steaming hot. Stir in rum flavoring. Serve warm and top each serving with dollup of whipped cream and dash of nutmeg. One cup rum may be substituted for rum flavoring. 12 servings.

FROSTED MALTED MILK

2/3 c. corn syrup
1/4 c. malted milk powder
2 eggs, beaten

1 c. milk
1 c. whipped cream

Combine all ingredients except whipped cream. Fold in whipped cream and freeze until mushy. Place in glasses and serve.

Frances Murray, Tullahoma, Tennessee

MOCK PINK CHAMPAGNE

1 1/2 c. sugar
3 c. water
3 c. grapefruit juice
2 c. orange juice
3/4 c. grenadine syrup

3 1-pt. 12-oz. bottles
   ginger ale, chilled
40 twists of lemon peel
40 maraschino cherries with
   stems

Combine the sugar and water in a saucepan. Bring to a boil and cook, stirring, for about 3 minutes or until sugar is dissolved and syrup forms. Cool. Combine the syrup, fruit juices and grenadine syrup and chill. Pour into a punch bowl and add ginger ale. Add several trays of ice cubes. Serve in champagne or sherbet glasses with lemon twist and cherry in each glass. 40 servings.

Mrs. Corliss Jones, Muskogee, Oklahoma

WITCHES' CAULDRON

1 qt. apple juice	1/4 tsp. nutmeg
6 cinnamon sticks	1 qt. chilled ginger ale
16 whole cloves	

Combine first 4 ingredients in a saucepan and bring to a boil. Simmer for 10 minutes and strain. Chill. Pour into a punch bowl and add ginger ale. Place pieces of dry ice in punch bowl to give smoking effect. 2 quarts.

Mrs. Erma Hamby, LaGrange, Kentucky

PIZZA FINGER SNACKS

1/2 lb. salami	1 sm. can tomato paste
1/2 lb. American cheese	2 lge. loaves sliced bread
1 lge. green pepper	Melted margarine
1 tbsp. Italian seasoning	

Grind the salami, cheese and green pepper together. Add Italian seasoning and tomato paste and mix well. Cut crusts off slices of bread and roll each slice thin with a rolling pin. Spread with cheese mixture. Roll each slice as for jelly roll and cut each roll in half. Refrigerate or freeze until ready to bake. Brush each roll with margarine and place on a greased cookie sheet. Bake in 375-degree oven for 15 to 20 minutes and serve hot. 50 servings.

Esther Lasker, Sarasota, Florida

DIABLO EGGS

6 hard-boiled eggs	2 tbsp. mayonnaise
1/2 tsp. chopped parsley	Dash of hot sauce
1 tsp. mustard	Salt and pepper to taste
1/4 c. minced onion	Paprika
1 tbsp. minced sweet pickles	

Cut the eggs in half lengthwise and remove egg yolks. Place yolks in a bowl and mash. Add the parsley, mustard, onion, pickles, mayonnaise, hot sauce, salt and pepper and mix well. Fill egg whites and sprinkle with paprika.

Mrs. Ed Karls, Phoenix, Arizona

Bavarian Chip Dip (below)

BAVARIAN CHIP DIP

1 3-oz. package cream
  cheese, softened
2 tbsp. lemon juice
1 8-oz. package
  braunschweiger

1 env. onion soup mix
1 tbsp. prepared horseradish
1 tsp. Worcestershire sauce
Dash of hot sauce
2/3 c. evaporated milk

Combine the cream cheese and lemon juice in an electric blender or small bowl of electric mixer. Add the braunschweiger, soup mix, horseradish, Worcestershire sauce, hot sauce and evaporated milk and blend or beat with mixer at high speed until smooth. Chill. 2 cups.

SMOKED EGG DIP

12 hard-cooked eggs, mashed
2 tbsp. soft margarine
1 1/2 tbsp. liquid smoke
1 tbsp. brown mustard
2 tsp. Worcestershire sauce

4 drops of hot sauce
1 tsp. salt
1/4 tsp. pepper
3/4 c. mayonnaise

Combine all ingredients in a bowl and beat until smooth. Refrigerate until chilled. Garnish with radish slices and serve with crackers, potato chips or melba toast.

Lucy Bearden, Eastman, Georgia

MEPHISTOPHELES DIP

2 lge. tomatoes, peeled
2 lge. ripe avocados,
  peeled

1 pt. cottage cheese
2 sm. cloves of garlic,
  pressed

1/4 green pepper, minced
1 sm. onion, minced
Juice of 1 lemon

2 dashes of hot sauce
Salt to taste

Mash the tomatoes and avocados together in a bowl and blend in remaining ingredients. Serve with crackers or corn chips.

Mrs. Jack Williams, Phoenix, Arizona

BACON AND SOUR CREAM DIP

1 8-oz. package cream
    cheese
3 tbsp. chopped chives
1 c. sour cream
1 tsp. horseradish

Dash of garlic salt
Dash of cayenne pepper
6 strips cooked bacon,
    crumbled

Have the cream cheese at room temperature. Blend the cream cheese with chives, sour cream, horseradish, garlic salt and cayenne pepper in a bowl. Stir in 2/3 of the bacon and place remaining bacon on top. 3 cups.

Kathy Loman, Wilmington, North Carolina

LOBSTER FONDUE

1 can frozen cream of
    shrimp soup, thawed
1/4 c. milk
1 7 1/2-oz. can lobster
2 tsp. lemon juice

1/2 c. shredded American
    process cheese
Dash of paprika
Dash of white pepper

Combine the soup and milk in fondue pot and cover. Heat through, stirring frequently. Drain and flake the lobster and add to soup mixture. Fold in remaining ingredients and heat through. Serve with melba toast. 2 3/4 cups.

Mrs. Stanley Krug, Scottsdale, Arizona

SWISS CHEESE-SHRIMP FONDUE

1 clove of garlic, halved
2 cans frozen shrimp soup
1 c. milk
1 lb. Swiss cheese, grated

Pepper and paprika to taste
Cooked cleaned shrimp
French bread, cut in 1-in.
    cubes

Rub fondue pot with garlic. Heat the soup in the pot, stirring until smooth. Add the milk slowly and mix well. Add the cheese and stir until melted. Sprinkle with pepper and paprika and place over flame. Place shrimp and bread on fondue forks and dip into cheese mixture. 6-8 servings.

Mrs. M. A. Barnes, West Columbia, South Carolina

Kraut-Meat Pasties (below)

KRAUT-MEAT PASTIES

2 1/2 c. sauerkraut	1/4 tsp. pepper
2 c. sifted flour	1/2 c. shortening
1/2 tsp. salt	Ground Meat Filling

Drain the sauerkraut well and reserve 2 tablespoons liquid. Sift the flour, salt and pepper together into a bowl and cut in the shortening. Add the sauerkraut and reserved liquid and toss with a fork until dry ingredients are moistened. Press together to form a ball. Roll out 1/8 of the pastry at a time on a well-floured pastry cloth to 8-inch circles. Place about 3/4 cup Ground Meat Filling in center of each circle and fold over. Seal edges and prick tops with a fork. Place on ungreased cookie sheets. Bake in 375-degree oven for 40 to 45 minutes or until lightly browned.

Ground Meat Filling

1/2 c. chopped onion	1 tsp. monosodium glutamate
1 tbsp. salad oil	1/2 tsp. marjoram leaves
1 lb. ground beef	1/4 tsp. pepper
1/2 lb. ground lean pork	1/2 c. Italian-style bread
1/2 lb. ground veal	crumbs
2 1/2 tsp. salt	

Saute the onion in salad oil until crisp-tender. Stir in meats and remaining ingredients except bread crumbs and cook, stirring, for about 5 minutes or until meats are light brown. Remove from heat and stir in the bread crumbs. Cool.

LONG BOY CHEESEBURGERS

3 7-in. brown-and-serve	1/4 c. catsup
French loaves	1/4 c. chopped onion
1 lb. ground beef	1/2 c. corn flake crumbs
1 tsp. salt	1/2 c. evaporated milk
1/4 tsp. pepper	Cheese slices
1 tbsp. Worcestershire sauce	

Cut the French loaves in half horizontally. Mix remaining ingredients except cheese and spread on cut sides of bread. Place on a cookie sheet. Bake at 375 degrees for 25 minutes. Cover with cheese slices and bake for 5 minutes longer. 6 servings.

Kelsey H. Ingle, Gainesville, Florida

GROUND BEEF WITH BEANS AND RICE

3/4 c. rice	2 c. stewed tomatoes
1 lb. ground beef	1 clove of garlic, minced
1/2 tsp. oregano	1 can kidney beans
1 tsp. minced onion	Worcestershire sauce to taste
1 tsp. salt	

Cook the rice according to package directions and set aside. Combine the ground beef, oregano, onion and salt in a large skillet and cook until beef is almost done. Add the tomatoes, garlic and kidney beans and cook for 15 minutes. Add rice and Worcestershire sauce and simmer for 5 minutes longer. 6 servings.

Mrs. J. L. Bissell, Gravette, Arkansas

SPAGHETTI AND MEATBALLS FOR A CROWD

3 lb. ground beef	3 c. bread crumbs
4 c. minced onions	6 eggs
6 cloves of garlic, minced	3 tbsp. salt
1 c. chopped parsley	3 tsp. pepper
3 c. grated Parmesan cheese	

Mix all ingredients in a bowl and add enough water to moisten. Shape into small balls and place in a single layer in a large baking pan. Bake at 450 degrees for 30 minutes.

Sauce and Spaghetti

5 c. chopped onion	2 1/2 tsp. dried thyme
10 cloves of garlic, minced	3 tbsp. salt
1/2 c. oil	1 tsp. pepper
5 28-oz. cans tomatoes	1 tsp. crushed red pepper
5 c. water	5 6-oz. cans tomato paste
1 c. chopped parsley	4 lb. spaghetti
1/2 tsp. dried basil	Grated Parmesan cheese

Cook the onion and garlic in oil in a large skillet for 5 minutes. Add remaining ingredients except spaghetti and cheese and simmer for 30 minutes. Pour over meatballs and cover. Bake at 350 degrees for 1 hour and 30 minutes. Cook the spaghetti according to package directions and drain well. Serve the meatballs and sauce over the spaghetti and top with Parmesan cheese.

Mrs. Annie G. Childress, Mangham, Louisiana

MEAT-SPAGHETTI CASSEROLE

1 lb. ground beef
1/2 lb. ground lean pork
1 c. diced onions
2 c. diced celery
1/2 lb. thin spaghetti, broken

1 c. cubed sharp cheese
1 4-oz. can mushrooms
1 can tomato soup
Salt and pepper to taste

Cook the beef and pork in frying pan, stirring and breaking apart, until brown. Add the onions and celery and cook until onions and celery are soft. Cook the spaghetti according to package directions and drain. Add the meat mixture, cheese, mushrooms, soup and seasonings and mix thoroughly. Turn into a large casserole. Bake at 350 degrees for 20 minutes. 6-8 servings.

Mrs. Roland P. Matchett, Covington, Kentucky

MACARONI WITH SAUSAGE-EGGPLANT SAUCE

1 2-lb. eggplant
3/4 lb. Italian hot sausage
3/4 lb. Italian sweet sausage
1 tbsp. olive oil
1/2 c. chopped onion
2 lge. cloves of garlic,
    crushed
2 8-oz. cans tomato sauce

1 28-oz. can plum
    tomatoes
1 tsp. crushed basil leaves
Salt
Pepper to taste
4 c. elbow macaroni
Grated Parmesan cheese (opt.)

Peel the eggplant and cut in 1/2-inch cubes. Remove casing from sausages and break sausages into chunks. Place sausages and 1/3 cup water in a Dutch oven and

Macaroni with Sausage-Eggplant Sauce (above)

cover. Cook for 10 minutes, stirring occasionally. Remove cover and drain off water. Saute until lightly browned and remove from Dutch oven. Add the olive oil to Dutch oven and heat. Stir in the onion and garlic and saute until lightly browned. Add sausages, eggplant, tomato sauce, tomatoes and basil and cover. Simmer for 45 minutes, stirring occasionally. Uncover and simmer for 15 minutes longer. Season with salt to taste and pepper. Add 2 tablespoons salt to 6 quarts boiling water in a large saucepan. Add macaroni gradually so that water continues to boil and cook, stirring occasionally, until tender. Drain in a colander. Serve macaroni with eggplant mixture and sprinkle with Parmesan cheese.

CHALUPES

1 lb. lean ground beef	1 pkg. frozen tortillas
4 tbsp. chili powder	Salt to taste
1 tbsp. oregano	2 tomatoes, sliced
2 tbsp. garlic salt	1 head lettuce, sliced
2 No. 303 cans refried beans	2 c. grated Cheddar cheese

Cook the beef in a saucepan until brown. Add the chili powder, oregano and garlic salt and stir until well blended. Drain off the grease. Add the beans and cook over low heat for 20 minutes. Fry tortillas in small amount of fat in a skillet until crisp and drain. Salt each tortilla. Serve beef mixture on tortillas and top each serving with tomatoes, lettuce and cheese. 6-8 servings.

Mildred Hill, Hillsboro, Texas

HOT MEAT SALAD

1/2 head lettuce, shredded	1 8-oz. can tomato sauce
1 tomato, diced	2 tbsp. chili powder
1 onion, chopped	Salt and pepper to taste
1 lb. ground beef	1 med. package corn chips

Combine the lettuce, tomato and onion in a bowl. Brown the ground beef in a skillet. Add the tomato sauce, chili powder, salt and pepper and cook until blended. Pour over lettuce mixture and toss. Add the corn chips and toss lightly. Serve immediately. 6 servings.

Mrs. Allen Daggett, Houston, Texas

DEVIL DOG KABOBS

1/3 c. brown sugar	Frankfurters, cut in
1/2 tsp. nutmeg	1-in. slices
2 tbsp. orange juice	Canned sm. onions
6 tbsp. melted butter	Apple slices

Combine first 4 ingredients in a bowl. Place the frankfurters, onions and apple slices in alternate layers on skewers. Broil over coals until heated through, basting frequently with sugar mixture.

Mrs. Paula Arnold, Charlotte, North Carolina

PIRATE'S POOR BOYS

6 sm. loaves French bread	3 hard-cooked eggs, sliced
Soft butter	6 slices mozzarella cheese
6 slices garlic salami	6 slices boiled ham
3 lge. tomatoes, thinly	6 slices roast beef
sliced	Seasoned salt to taste
6 slices Swiss cheese	Savory to taste

Cut loaves of bread in half horizontally and remove soft centers. Spread butter on bottom halves of bread. Place 1 slice salami, 1 slice tomato, 1 slice Swiss cheese, 1 slice egg, 1 slice tomato, 1 slice mozzarella cheese, 1 slice ham, 1 slice tomato, 1 slice egg and 1 slice roast beef in overlapping layers on each loaf. Butter top halves of bread and sprinkle with seasoned salt and savory. Join halves. Wrap in aluminum foil and seal securely, leaving at least 1-inch hollow space along length of bread. Place on low coals for 10 minutes, turning once. Open foil and turn back. Cook for 5 to 10 minutes longer or until bread is lightly browned. Sliced turkey or chicken may be substituted for roast beef.

Mrs. Sandra Raines, Vernon, Florida

STUFFED HARD ROLLS

4 or 5 hard dinner rolls	3 tbsp. sweet pickle relish
1 c. butter	2 tbsp. grated onion
1 8-oz. package cream	1/2 c. chopped walnuts
cheese	1 c. ground salami or ham
1 tbsp. Worcestershire sauce	2 tsp. anchovy paste (opt.)
1/2 tsp. curry powder	3 tbsp. capers (opt.)

Remove ends from rolls and remove soft centers. Cream the butter with cream cheese until smooth. Add remaining ingredients and mix well. Pack into rolls and refrigerate overnight. Slice and arrange on serving tray.

Mrs. John Abbott, Newark, Delaware

MOIST CHOCOLATE CAKE

2 tsp. soda	2 eggs
1 c. boiling water	2 1/2 c. flour
2 1/2 c. sugar	1/2 tsp. salt
3/4 c. oil	1 c. sour milk or buttermilk
1/2 c. cocoa	1 tsp. vanilla

Dissolve soda in boiling water and cool. Place remaining ingredients in a bowl and mix well. Add soda mixture and beat until mixed. Pour into greased 12 x 9-inch baking pan. Bake at 350 degrees for 30 minutes or until done.

Janice Langley, De Quincy, Louisiana

WITCH HAT COOKIES

2 c. sifted flour	1 c. sugar
1/3 c. instant nonfat dry milk	1 egg
1 tsp. baking powder	1 tsp. vanilla
3/4 tsp. salt	2 tbsp. water
1/2 c. shortening	2 sq. unsweetened chocolate
	Confectioners' sugar frosting

Sift the flour, milk, baking powder and salt together. Cream the shortening in a bowl and add sugar gradually, beating until light and fluffy. Beat in egg and stir in the vanilla and water. Add dry ingredients gradually, beating until smooth. Melt the chocolate over hot water and cool. Stir into flour mixture. Divide dough into 3 portions and chill for several hours. Roll each portion out 1/8 inch thick on lightly floured board. Cut in witch hat shape, using cardboard with hat shape for guide. Place on well-greased cookie sheet. Bake at 400 degrees for about 10 minutes. Remove from cookie sheet and cool. Place frosting in a pastry tube and pipe children's names onto cookies.

Mrs. Nancy Threatt, Columbia, South Carolina

CARAMEL APPLES

1 14-oz. can sweetened condensed milk	1/8 tsp. salt
1 c. sugar	1 tsp. vanilla
1/2 c. light corn syrup	6 med. apples

Mix the milk, sugar, corn syrup and salt in a heavy 2-quart saucepan. Cook over low heat, stirring constantly, until mixture comes to a boil and sugar is dissolved. Cook over low heat, stirring constantly, to 230 degrees on a candy thermometer or until mixture spins a 2-inch thread when dropped from spoon. Remove from heat. Stir in the vanilla and cool for 5 minutes. Insert wooden skewers in apples and dip into caramel mixture until well covered, tilting pan as needed. Cool on waxed paper or a lightly greased baking sheet.

Caramel Apples (above)

129

NEVER-FAIL FIVE-MINUTE FUDGE

2/3 c. evaporated milk	16 marshmallows, diced
1 2/3 c. sugar	1 1/2 c. chocolate or
1/2 tsp. salt	caramel chips
1/2 c. chopped nuts	1 tsp. vanilla

Mix the milk, sugar and salt in a saucepan and place over low heat. Bring to boiling point and cook for 5 minutes, stirring constantly. Remove from heat. Add the nuts, marshmallows, chocolate chips and vanilla and stir for 1 to 2 minutes or until marshmallows are melted. Pour into a greased 9-inch pan and cool. Cut into squares.

Mrs. James Richard, Middletown, Virginia

BEWITCHING RAISIN DUNKERS

1 c. sifted flour	2 1/2 tbsp. shortening
Sugar	1/3 c. milk
1 1/2 tsp. baking powder	1/3 c. chopped seedless
1/2 tsp. salt	raisins
Cinnamon	1/4 c. melted butter

Sift the flour, 2 tablespoons sugar, baking powder, salt and 1/8 teaspoon cinnamon together into a bowl and cut in shortening until mixture is size of small peas. Add milk and raisins and stir until mixed. Place on lightly floured board and roll out to 1/4 inch thickness. Cut in 1/2 x 6-inch strips. Fold strips in half and twist. Place on baking sheet. Bake at 425 degrees for about 12 minutes or until lightly browned. Mix 1/4 cup sugar and 1/4 teaspoon cinnamon. Dip twists in butter and roll in sugar mixture. Serve warm.

Mrs. Harry Foster, Lexington, Kentucky

ORANGE-COCONUT BALLS

1 12-oz. box vanilla wafers	1 box powdered sugar
1 stick margarine, softened	1 c. chopped nuts
1 6-oz. can frozen orange	1 pkg. flaked coconut
juice concentrate, thawed	

Crush the vanilla wafers and place in a bowl. Add remaining ingredients except coconut and mix until blended. Shape in small balls and roll in coconut.

Mrs. Dorothy T. Rabb, Minden, Louisiana

FROSTED PUMPKIN DOUGHNUTS

2 eggs	1 tsp. soda
1 c. sugar	1/2 tsp. salt
2 tbsp. butter, softened	1/2 tsp. cinnamon
1 c. canned pumpkin	1/2 tsp. nutmeg
4 c. sifted flour	1 tbsp. lemon juice
2 tsp. baking powder	1 c. evaporated milk

Combine the eggs, sugar and butter in a large mixing bowl and blend with electric mixer. Beat in pumpkin. Sift dry ingredients together. Mix the lemon juice and milk. Add dry ingredients to sugar mixture alternately with milk mixture, beginning and ending with dry ingredients and beating well after each addition. Cover and chill for 2 hours. Turn out onto a well-floured pastry board and knead 5 or 6 times. Roll out to 1/4-inch thickness and cut with a floured doughnut cutter. Fry in deep fat at 375 degrees for 3 to 4 minutes or until golden, turning once. Drain on absorbent paper. Frost with orange frosting or sprinkle with powdered sugar.

Orange Frosting

3 c. (about) confectioners' sugar	2 tbsp. orange juice
	1 tbsp. evaporated milk
1 tsp. grated orange rind	

Combine all ingredients in a bowl and beat until smooth. Spread on warm doughnuts. 2 dozen.

Photograph for this recipe on page 116.

GLAZED DOUGHNUTS

2 c. scalded milk	2 eggs, beaten
1/2 c. shortening	6 c. flour
1/2 c. sugar	1 box powdered sugar
2 tsp. salt	2/3 c. boiling water
1 pkg. yeast	

Mix the milk, shortening, sugar and salt in a bowl and cool to lukewarm. Add yeast and eggs and mix well. Add flour and stir well. Cover and let rise until doubled in bulk. Roll out on lightly floured board and cut with a doughnut cutter. Let rise for 45 minutes. Fry in deep, hot fat until brown and drain on absorbent paper. Mix powdered sugar and water and dip warm doughnuts in powdered sugar mixture. Drain on rack placed over cookie sheet.

Mrs. Stephen Knight, Oak Ridge, Tennessee

BLACK SORCERY FONDUE

2 tbsp. light corn syrup	1/4 c. finely chopped pecans
1/2 c. light cream	1 tsp. vanilla
1 9-oz. bar milk chocolate, broken	Bite-sized chunks of cake, fruits or marshmallows

Heat the syrup and cream in a fondue pot over flame. Stir in the chocolate and heat, stirring constantly, until chocolate is melted. Stir in pecans and vanilla. Place cake on fondue forks and twirl in chocolate mixture. Cool slightly.

Mrs. Phoebe Cox, Fairmont, West Virginia

Country-Baked Turkey (page 144)

thanksgiving

Thanksgiving down South comes in the quiet time after the harvest is in, when the land lies resting under grey skies that promise a winter full of rains and damp fogs. In the midst of this peace excited families plan their annual gathering for Thanksgiving Dinner.

The spirit of this holiday is a wonderfully warm one as people give thanks for their bounty during the year which is passing . . . a bounty which included not just material prosperity but the love we all have for one another.

Remember the family Thanksgiving dinners of your childhood? The long ride to Grandmother's. The excitement of seeing relatives you hadn't seen since last Thanksgiving. The quiet joy of the church service followed by the riotous excitement of a local football game. Yes, these things are all part of our Thanksgiving heritage.

To help you recapture that heritage and give it new meaning, *Southern Living* homemakers share their favorite Thanksgiving recipes with you. From the menu on page 7 to the delicious recipes you'll find in the following pages, this is a section that will add new sparkle to your Thanksgiving holiday dinner party. Every recipe is a tried-and-proven family-pleasing food certain to bring you sincere compliments from those who share your Thanksgiving Dinner. Serve them to your family and guests — and enjoy the results!

133

Dining tables in southern homes were once called "groaning boards" because when they were loaded with food for one of the almost legendary southern dinners, they literally groaned! And one glance at the menu on page 7 will tell you why.

When you serve this menu, you begin with Hot Spiced Vineyard Cup . . . Smoked Salmon . . . Cream of Pumpkin Soup . . . Harvest Apple Salad . . . and Virginia Sweet Pickles. Our menu includes Golden Roast Turkey with Dressing and Gravy and Corn Souffle, both popular favorites in southern homes. Sweet Potato-Stuffed Apples is another highly prized southern dish and one certain to delight your family. Finish your Thanksgiving dinner with a flourish — serve Spicy Squash Pie — and your family will learn exactly what was meant by a "groaning board!"

entertaining
FOR THANKSGIVING

Whether you choose to serve the suggested menu or to create your own with delicious recipes from the section that follows, an important part of your holiday will be your family's Thanksgiving traditions. One of the very nicest southern customs is that of sharing the year's bounty. This sharing may take the form of an invitation to a stranger to share the family's dinner . . . baskets overflowing with special foods to be given to those less fortunate . . . or simply a warmhearted family gathering around the Thanksgiving table. But sharing is central to this holiday. Perhaps your family can think of other ways to share its bounty with people, and they'll be delighted to discover how much sharing can add to *your* holiday.

If you want to really say "Happy Thanksgiving" in an extra-special way, mail invitations to your Dinner a week or so in advance. They establish the party atmosphere immediately. And do say "greetings and happy holiday" with decorations around your front door. Try piling up golden pumpkins . . . mixing great piles of autumn leaves . . . or tying Indian corn to your door knocker.

Spread Thanksgiving cheer inside your home, too. In many southern homes, a blazing fire is lit early in the morning and kept going all day long. Thoughtful southern homemakers know that few things make guests feel more welcome than coming from the cold outdoors into a room with a fire burning brightly. If you don't have a fireplace, you might warm your guests with fresh coffee or holiday punch. Do keep some on hand all day to offer those friends and neighbors who drop in to visit. And brighten your home still further by placing fresh-cut seasonal flowers or sprays of berries in your very best vases and scattering them on tabletops throughout the house.

Continue the harvest-holiday theme with your table decorations. The most time-honored of all Thanksgiving decorations is the horn of plenty — or cornucopia — overflowing with the richness of the harvest. Pile it full of fruits, vegetables, and nuts, and let them spill out onto the table. If you don't have a horn, try turning a wooden bucket on its side and filling it as you would a cornucopia.

If your Thanksgiving party is a buffet, try a yellow and gold color scheme on your buffet table. Make tiny pumpkins from cheese — golden ripe Cheddar is particularly good. Cluster chrysanthemums into vases so that they appear to be pompons. Have dishes of gleaming tangerines on the table along with jellied cranberry . . . walnuts . . . raisins . . . and plump, pale yellow mushrooms.

A particularly elegant — and appropriate — centerpiece is frosted fruit. Dip pieces of fruit into egg whites which have been beaten until they are frothy. Then dip the damp fruit into granulated sugar and set it on a wire rack until it is dry. This fruit is particularly eye-appealing when massed in a glass bowl or compote and set between pairs of tall candles.

Let the children participate in the holiday fun and excitement by making place cards for the big dinner. Provide a quiet place to work, old shirts for smocks, scissors (blunt ones, please), glue, construction paper, crayons, and a printed list of your guests' names. Children feel so proud when they are given a part in holiday festivities, and their occupation will give grown-ups time to visit and catch up on the year's news.

As hostess, you can join your guests' conversations by planning your meal carefully. Try serving the first course in the living room and saving the table for the main course. To cut down on your work, arrange the main course in pretty serving dishes on a buffet or sideboard and let your guests help themselves. You might even want to try a two-table Thanksgiving feast. Adults eat at a big table decorated with the very best china, sterling, and crystal. At a smaller, scaled-down table the children eat, in full view of and participating with the adults but with plastic tablecloth and sturdier table service.

When the feast has ended, make things as easy as possible on yourself. Enlist helpers from the younger guests and let them clean up the tables and wash and dry the dishes. Perhaps you'll plan an autumn walk in the crisp after-noon air . . . a game of touch football . . . a quiet afternoon of television viewing. Thanksgiving Day is often the time when major networks show special holiday programs — a delight for people of all ages!

Supper? plan a meal of leftover turkey and vegetables served on paper plates. No cooking, no fuss, and best of all, no dishes to wash.

All the recipes you'll need to plan an extra-special, southern-style Thanks-giving are in the pages that follow. Couple them with your own imaginative way of decorating your home and serving your foods, and you'll be certain to have a most memorable holiday!

HOT SPICED VINEYARD CUP

1 qt. grape juice	Juice and grated rind of 1
2 c. boiling water	lemon
1/2 c. sugar	Juice and grated rind of 1
2 nutmegs, cracked	orange
1 1/2 sticks cinnamon	Lemon slices

Combine all ingredients except lemon slices in a saucepan and bring to a boil, stirring until sugar is dissolved. Reduce heat and simmer for 15 minutes. Strain. Float a lemon slice in each cup and garnish with a cherry. 8 servings.

Mrs. Moses B. Daniels, Wilson, North Carolina

HUNTERS' COFFEE

8 c. strong coffee	Ground nutmeg or cinnamon
Sugar to taste	8 brandied cherries
Rum extract to taste	8 cinnamon sticks

Pour steaming hot coffee into mugs. Add sugar, rum extract and a sprinkle of nutmeg. Garnish with a cherry and serve with a cinnamon stick stirrer.

Mrs. James Sharp, Pascagoula, Mississippi

SMOKED SALMON

1/2 lb. smoked salmon	Thin dark bread slices
Sprigs of parsley	Butter
Lemon wedges	Olive oil
Capers	

Cut smoked salmon into paper-thin slices and arrange on a chilled platter with parsley, lemon wedges and capers. Spread bread with butter and place around edge of platter. Serve with olive oil.

Mrs. G. H. Anderson, Baton Rouge, Louisiana

OYSTERS ON THE HALF SHELL

3 doz. oysters in shells	Lemon wedges
Pepper to taste	

Open the oysters and leave the oysters loose in bottom half of the shell. Arrange 6 opened oysters on a bed of finely chopped ice for each serving. Sprinkle with pepper and garnish with lemon wedge. Place a small dish of horseradish or cocktail sauce in the middle of each plate, if desired.

Mrs. Dolph Beaseley, Fort Smith, Arkansas

CREAM OF PUMPKIN SOUP

1 c. sliced green onion
1/4 c. plus 2 tbsp. melted
    butter or margarine
4 c. cooked mashed pumpkin
2   10 3/4-oz. cans chicken
    broth, undiluted

2 small tomatoes, peeled and
    chopped
1 tsp. salt
Dash of pepper
2 c. half-and-half

Saute onion in butter until tender. Add remaining ingredients except half-and-half. Cover and simmer 10 minutes, stirring occasionally. Place half of the mixture in blender container and process until smooth. Repeat blending with remaining soup. Add half-and-half and heat through. Serve warm. 12 to 15 small servings.

Photograph for this recipe on page 149.

FRUIT SOUP

1/2 lb. prunes
1/4 lb. dried apricots
1 c. seedless raisins
4 tbsp. tapioca
1 c. sugar
1 stick cinnamon

3 apples, diced
1 lemon, sliced
1 orange, sliced
1/4 tsp. salt
1/4 c. maraschino cherries

Place the prunes, apricots, raisins and tapioca in a saucepan and cover with water. Soak overnight. Combine all ingredients except cherries in 2 quarts water and cook until fruits are soft, adding water or grape juice, if needed. Serve hot or cold and garnish with the cherries. Use the large variety of tapioca for this recipe. One pint canned apricots may be substituted for the dried apricots.

Fruit Soup (above)

AUTUMN VEGETABLE SALAD

2 env. unflavored gelatin	1 c. shredded cabbage
3/4 c. water	1 c. shredded carrots
1/2 c. white wine vinegar	1/2 c. finely chopped celery
2 tbsp. sugar	1/2 c. finely chopped
2 tsp. seasoned salt	radishes
3 to 4 drops of hot sauce	1 tbsp. finely chopped
1 1-pt. 2-oz. can pineapple	green onion
juice	2 tbsp. chopped pimento

Soften the gelatin in water in a saucepan. Add the vinegar, sugar, salt and hot sauce and heat, stirring, until gelatin is dissolved. Add pineapple juice and chill until partially set. Fold in remaining ingredients and spoon into individual molds or 5-cup ring mold. Chill until firm. Unmold and serve on salad greens. Garnish with mayonnaise. 8 servings.

Mrs. J. W. Hopkins, Abilene, Texas

CARROT AND CELERY SALAD

1 env. unflavored gelatin	1/4 c. lemon juice
1/4 c. sugar	1 1/2 c. grated carrots
1/2 tsp. salt	1/4 c. finely diced celery
1 1/2 c. water	1/4 c. diced green pepper

Mix the gelatin, sugar and salt and stir in 1/2 cup water. Place over low heat, stirring constantly, until gelatin is dissolved. Remove from heat and stir in remaining water and lemon juice. Chill until partially set. Fold in remaining ingredients and turn into 3-cup mold or individual molds. Chill until firm. Unmold and serve on salad greens. 6 servings.

Mattie Mary Green, Neely, Mississippi

CRANBERRY RING MOLD WITH OLD-FASHIONED MAYONNAISE

1 3-oz. package raspberry	1/2 c. crushed pineapple,
gelatin	drained
2 tsp. lemon juice	1/2 c. diced celery
1 c. whole cranberry sauce	

Dissolve the gelatin in 1 cup hot water in a bowl. Add 1/2 cup cold water and lemon juice and chill until slightly thickened. Fold in the cranberry sauce, pineapple and celery and pour into ring mold. Chill until firm.

Old-Fashioned Mayonnaise

1 tbsp. sugar	1/2 c. water
1 tbsp. flour	2 tbsp. butter
1/2 tsp. dry mustard	2 eggs, beaten
1 tsp. salt	1/2 c. milk
1/2 c. vinegar	1/2 c. chopped nuts

Combine the sugar, flour, mustard, salt, vinegar and water in a saucepan and bring to boiling point over low heat, stirring constantly. Add the butter, eggs and milk and cook for about 3 minutes, stirring. Remove from heat and beat well. Serve over salad and garnish with nuts. 6 servings.

Mrs. Mack Thurman, Waycross, Georgia

HARVEST APPLE SALAD

1 3-oz. package lemon
   gelatin
1 c. hot water
1 1-lb. can sweetened
   applesauce
1/2 tsp. salt

1 tbsp. lemon juice
1/2 c. chopped red pickled
   crab apples
1 sm. package cream cheese,
   cut in cubes

Dissolve the gelatin in hot water in a bowl. Stir in the applesauce, salt and lemon juice and chill until slightly thickened. Fold in remaining ingredients and chill until firm.

Mrs. John Dimmick, Winston-Salem, North Carolina

APRICOT SURPRISE RING

1 1-lb. 4-oz. can apricot
   halves
1 3-oz. package orange
   gelatin

1/2 c. water
1/3 c. small curd cottage
   cheese
1 c. evaporated skimmed milk

Drain the apricots and reserve syrup. Pour the reserved syrup into a saucepan and bring to boiling point. Add the gelatin and stir until dissolved. Stir in the water and cool. Fill apricot halves with cottage cheese and place 2 halves together. Place in a 5 1/2-cup ring mold. Stir the milk into gelatin mixture and pour over apricots. Chill until firm. 6 servings.

Apricot Surprise Ring (above)

Ginger-Peach Conserve (below), Spiced Melon Balls (page 141)

GINGER-PEACH CONSERVE

1 12-oz. package frozen sliced peaches, thawed	**1/2 c. coarsely chopped walnuts**
1/4 c. sugar	**2 tbsp. finely chopped crystallized ginger**
1/2 tsp. ground cinnamon	**1/4 c. maraschino cherries**

Drain the peaches and reserve juice. Mix reserved juice with the sugar and cinnamon in a small bowl and stir until sugar is dissolved. Pour over the peaches. Add the walnuts, ginger and cherries and mix well. Chill until ready to serve. 2 1/2 cups.

VIRGINIA SWEET PICKLES

Cider vinegar	**9 c. sugar**
1 1-lb. 9-oz. box salt	**1/3 c. pickling spices**
Cucumbers	**1 tbsp. celery seed**
3 tbsp. powdered alum	

Pour 1 gallon water into a kettle and bring to a boil. Add 1 tablespoon vinegar and salt and cool. Pour into a crock and add enough cucumbers to fill crock to within 3 inches of top. Let set for several days to 1 week. Drain and cut cucumbers in half or prick with a fork. Combine 1 gallon water and 1 tablespoon alum and pour over cucumbers. Let set for 1 day, then drain. Repeat process for 2 more days. Combine 6 cups vinegar, 5 cups sugar, pickling spices and celery seed in a saucepan and bring to a boil. Pour over the cucumbers and let set overnight. Drain vinegar mixture into a saucepan. Add 2 cups sugar and heat to boiling point. Pour over cucumbers and let set overnight. Drain vinegar mixture into a saucepan. Add remaining sugar and heat to boiling point. Place cucumbers in sterilized jars and pour vinegar mixture over cucumbers. Add tops to jars and process in hot water bath for 10 minutes.

Mrs. Bill Owen, Tuscaloosa, Alabama

SPICED MELON BALLS

2 12-oz. packages frozen
    melon balls, thawed
1/4 c. (firmly packed) light
    brown sugar

1/4 c. cider vinegar
5 or 6 whole cloves
1 cinnamon stick

Drain the melon balls and reserve juice. Combine reserved juice, brown sugar, vinegar, cloves and cinnamon in a saucepan and simmer for 5 minutes. Pour over the melon balls and cool. Chill until ready to serve. 3 cups.

CANTALOUPE PICKLES

2 cantaloupes
1 1/2 tsp. powdered alum
4 1/2 c. sugar

2 c. vinegar
1 lemon, sliced thin
1 tbsp. pickling spices

Cut cantaloupes into 12 lengthwise pieces. Remove seeds and peel. Place in enamel preserving kettle and cover with cold water. Add the alum, stir and cover. Let set overnight. Drain cantaloupes and rinse in cold water. Cover with cold water and bring to a boil. Reduce heat and simmer for about 20 minutes or until just tender. Drain. Mix the sugar, vinegar, 1/2 cup water and lemon and bring to a boil. Add to the cantaloupe and cook for about 1 hour or until cantaloupe is transparent. Add spices and cook for 15 minutes. Pack in sterilized jars and seal.

Mrs. M. Callis, Orlando, Florida

PICKLED HOT PODS

2 lb. tender fresh okra
5 pods hot pepper
5 cloves of garlic, peeled
1 qt. white vinegar

1/2 c. water
8 tbsp. salt
1 tbsp. celery or mustard
    seed (opt.)

Wash the okra and pack in 5 hot, sterilized pint jars, adding 1 pepper pod and 1 garlic clove to each jar. Mix remaining ingredients in a saucepan and bring to a boil. Pour over okra and seal. Let stand for several weeks before serving and chill for crispness.

Mrs. George N. Phillips, Dallas, Texas

BEET AND CABBAGE RELISH

1 qt. chopped cooked beets
1 qt. chopped cabbage
1 c. chopped onions
1 tbsp. salt

1 tbsp. prepared horseradish
1 1/2 c. sugar
3 c. vinegar

Combine all ingredients in a kettle and bring to a boil. Reduce heat and simmer for 10 minutes. Bring to a boil and pack into sterilized jars to within 1/8 inch of top. Seal the jars.

Mrs. Patty Thomas, Montgomery, Alabama

CABBAGE RELISH

4 lb. cabbage	4 c. sugar
9 lge. red bell peppers	2 1/2 pt. cider vinegar
9 lge. green bell peppers	1/2 c. water
8 lge. Bermuda onions	2 tbsp. celery seed
4 med. carrots	2 tbsp. mustard seed
1/2 c. salt	

Grind the cabbage, red and green peppers, onions and carrots and place in an enamel kettle. Add the salt and blend lightly. Cover and let stand for 6 hours. Place in a cheesecloth bag. Suspend and drain overnight. Place in a large container. Mix the sugar, vinegar, water, celery seed and mustard seed and pour over cabbage mixture. Blend well and place in sterilized jars, filling to within 1/2 inch of top. Add vinegar solution, if necessary, to cover top of relish. Cap the jars. Will keep for several months in cool place or refrigerator. 6-8 pints.

Florence Austin, Dallas, Texas

IOWA CORN RELISH

20 ears of corn	1 1/2 tbsp. mustard seed
1 c. chopped green pepper	2 tbsp. salt
1 c. chopped red pepper	1 tsp. celery seed
1 1/4 c. chopped onion	1 tsp. turmeric
1 c. chopped celery	1 qt. white vinegar
2 c. sugar	

Place the corn in a kettle and cover with boiling water. Boil for 5 minutes, then drain and plunge into cold water. Cut kernels from cobs and place in the kettle. Add remaining ingredients and simmer for 20 minutes. Pack into clean, hot pint jars to within 1 inch of top and making certain vinegar solution covers vegetables. Add lids. Process in pressure canner at 5 pounds pressure for 5 minutes or in hot water bath for 15 minutes. 6-7 pints.

Mrs. Edward Thompkin, Fort Smith, Oklahoma

SWEET ROASTED PORK

1 5-lb. pork loin roast	1 c. ginger ale
1 1-lb. 4-oz. jar apricot preserves	1/8 tsp. ginger
	1/8 tsp. pepper (opt.)
1/3 c. strained honey	1 1-lb. 13-oz. can whole apricots
1/4 c. lemon juice	
1/4 c. soy sauce	1 tbsp. grated lemon rind
1/2 clove of garlic, minced	1/4 c. grated coconut
1 sm. onion, minced	Parsley sprigs

Remove bone from roast and tie roast with string. Place in a dish. Combine 1/2 of the apricot preserves, the honey, lemon juice, soy sauce, garlic, onion, ginger ale, ginger and pepper and pour over roast. Marinate for 4 to 5 hours, turning occasionally. Remove roast from marinade and reserve marinade. Insert meat thermometer in roast and place roast on spit. Cook over low coals for about 3 hours and 30 minutes or to 185 degrees on meat thermometer, basting frequently with reserved marinade. Spread with half the remaining apricot preserves and grill for 5 minutes longer. Heat remaining marinade with remaining apricot preserves and serve over roast. Heat apricots with lemon rind. Remove roast to hot serving platter. Garnish with apricots and sprinkle with coconut and parsley sprigs. 6-8 servings.

Mrs. D. G. Cooper, Bisbee, Arizona

CALYPSO PORK AND YAMS

1 4 to 5-lb. pork loin roast, cracked	1/2 tsp. ground cloves
Garlic salt and pepper to taste	1/4 tsp. salt
1 1/4 c. dark corn syrup	1/4 c. butter or margarine
3 tbsp. dark rum (opt.)	6 med. cooked yams, peeled
1 tbsp. lemon juice	1/4 c. halved red maraschino cherries
1 tsp. ground ginger	1/2 c. cashew nuts

Score the fat side of pork roast and sprinkle all sides with garlic salt and pepper. Place on rack in a shallow roasting pan. Roast in 325-degree oven for 35 minutes per pound or until meat thermometer registers 170 degrees. Mix the corn syrup, rum, lemon juice, spices and salt for glaze. Combine 2/3 cup glaze with butter in a saucepan and heat through. Cut the yams in quarters and place in a shallow baking dish. Pour hot glaze mixture over the yams and sprinkle cherries and cashew nuts on top. Use remaining glaze to brush on pork frequently during last hour of roasting time. Bake yams with pork during last 30 minutes of roasting time, basting once or twice with glaze. Two 23-ounce cans yams, drained, may be substituted for cooked yams. 6 servings.

Calypso Pork and Yams (above)

COUNTRY-BAKED TURKEY

1 turkey	**1 recipe stuffing**
Salt to taste	**Melted butter**

Season the body and neck cavities of turkey with salt and fill with stuffing. Secure openings. Place the turkey on a rack in a roasting pan, breast side up. Brush with butter and cover neck cavity with foil. Bake at 400 degrees for 1 hour, basting turkey with pan drippings, then cover with lid or foil. Reduce temperature to 325 degrees and bake until turkey is tender.

Photograph for this recipe on page 132.

TURKEY WITH DRESSING AND GRAVY

1 10 to 12-lb. frozen turkey, thawed	**2 tsp. salt**
	2 tbsp. margarine

Remove giblets from turkey and reserve. Rinse turkey inside and out with cold water and drain. Sprinkle salt over the turkey and rub the turkey with margarine. Place in a roaster and add reserved giblets and 2 cups water. Cover top of turkey with foil and add roaster cover. Bake at 325 degrees for 4 hours or until leg is fork-tender. Remove the cover and baste turkey with drippings. Bake for about 30 minutes longer or until golden brown. Remove giblets and dice. Drain and reserve drippings.

Dressing

4 qt. day-old bread crumbs	**1 tsp. sage**
4 c. corn bread crumbs	**1/2 c. diced celery**
1/2 tsp. parsley flakes	**1/2 c. diced onion**
Salt to taste	**1/2 c. melted margarine**
1 tsp. pepper	**4 eggs**
1 tbsp. poultry seasoning	

Mix all ingredients well, adding reserved drippings and water, if needed, until very moist. Spoon into a baking dish. Bake at 350 degrees for about 40 minutes or until browned.

Giblet Gravy

1 tbsp. shortening	**1/4 tsp. pepper**
2 tbsp. flour	**2 c. water**
1/2 tsp. salt	

Heat the shortening in a skillet or saucepan. Add the flour and cook until brown. Add salt, pepper and giblets. Add the water and cook until thick, stirring constantly. Serve over dressing.

Mrs. Charles R. Jackson, Hopkinsville, Kentucky

ROAST TURKEY WITH CRANBERRY-STUFFED ORANGES

1 12-lb. turkey	1/2 tsp. hot sauce
Salt	1/2 tsp. poultry seasoning
Pepper to taste	8 c. bread cubes
Melted butter	2 tbsp. chopped parsley
1 c. chopped onions	Turkey or chicken broth
1 c. diced celery	

Rub the turkey cavity with salt to taste and pepper and rub the skin with melted butter. Combine 1/2 cup melted butter, onions, celery, hot sauce, poultry seasoning and 1 1/2 teaspoons salt in a heavy frypan and cook until onions are tender but not brown. Add the bread cubes and parsley and stir until thoroughly blended. Add enough broth to moisten to desired consistency. Fill turkey cavity loosely with stuffing mixture. Place the turkey in a large baking pan. Bake at 325 degrees for 6 to 7 hours or until done, basting occasionally with butter and pan drippings.

Cranberry-Stuffed Oranges

2 c. water	1 lb. cranberries
2 c. sugar	9 oranges

Combine the water and sugar in a saucepan and stir until sugar is dissolved. Bring to a boil and boil for 5 minutes. Wash the cranberries and drain. Add to the syrup and simmer without stirring until cranberries are tender. Skim foam from top. Cut off tops of the oranges and scoop out about 1/2 of the pulp. Place oranges in a baking dish, then place in the oven with the turkey. Bake for 1 hour and 30 minutes. Fill oranges with cranberry sauce just before serving. Place the turkey and oranges on a platter and garnish with fresh mint or parsley.

Roast Turkey with Cranberry-Stuffed Oranges (above)

ROAST PHEASANT

1 c. corn bread crumbs	Chopped apple to taste
1 c. biscuit crumbs	1 c. bulk sausage
Chicken bouillon	1 pheasant
Salt and pepper to taste	Ginger to taste
Sage to taste	Strips of bacon
1 sm. onion, chopped	

Combine the corn bread crumbs and biscuit crumbs with enough chicken bouillon to moisten well. Add the salt, pepper, sage, onion, apple and sausage and mix well. Stuff cavity of pheasant with dressing and rub pheasant with ginger. Place pheasant in a baking pan and place strips of bacon across breast. Cover with a damp cloth. Bake in 325-degree oven until pheasant is tender.

Mrs. Abb McKnight, Campbellsville, Kentucky

BAKED WILD DUCKS IN RED SAUCE

2 wild ducks	1/2 c. catsup
2 tbsp. salad oil	2 tbsp. lemon juice
1/4 c. grated onion	Salt to taste
1/4 tsp. paprika	1/4 c. cider vinegar
2 tbsp. brown sugar	4 tbsp. Worcestershire sauce

Rub ducks with oil. Mix remaining ingredients and brush half the mixture on ducks. Wrap ducks in foil and place in shallow baking pan. Bake at 325 degrees for 1 hour or until ducks are tender. Turn foil back and brush ducks with remaining sauce. Bake until brown.

Ann Elsie Schmetzer, Madisonville, Kentucky

THANKSGIVING ROAST DUCKLING

1 5 to 6-lb. dressed duckling	3/4 to 1 c. firmly packed light
1 tsp. salt	brown sugar
10 slices white bread, diced	1 egg, slightly beaten
1 1/2 c. peeled, chopped apple	2 tsp. grated orange rind
1 c. chopped walnuts	1 tsp. salt
1/2 c. chopped celery	1/4 tsp. pepper
1 c. orange juice	Celery leaves (opt.)

Rub cavity of duckling with 1 teaspoon salt. Combine remaining ingredients except celery leaves, and stir until well moistened. Stuff dressing into cavity of duckling. Spoon remaining dressing into a shallow casserole and set aside. Close cavity of duckling with skewers. Place duckling, breast side up, on rack in a shallow roasting pan. Bake, uncovered, at 425 degrees for 20 minutes. Lower heat to 325 degrees, and bake 2 hours or until drumsticks and thighs move easily. Bake extra stuffing at 325 degrees for 30 minutes. Serve duckling on platter garnished with celery leaves, if desired. 6 to 8 servings.

Photograph for this recipe on page 2.

ROAST GOOSE WITH PICKLE-SPICED STUFFING

1 8-oz. package herb-seasoned stuffing mix	1/4 c. butter
	1/2 tsp. ground sage
3 c. cooked rice	1 9-lb. goose
2 med. oranges, sectioned	Salt to taste
1 c. chopped cranberries	1 1/2 c. orange juice
1 c. chopped sweet mixed pickles	2 tbsp. light corn syrup
	1/2 c. orange marmalade
1/4 c. sweet pickle liquid	

Mix the stuffing mix, rice, orange sections, cranberries, pickles, pickle liquid, butter and sage in a large bowl. Stuff neck cavity of goose with stuffing and skewer or sew skin to back of goose. Rub inside of goose with salt and fill with stuffing. Close with skewers or sew. Place on rack in a shallow roasting pan. Bake in 325-degree oven for 2 hours, then drain off fat. Combine 1 cup orange juice and corn syrup and brush over goose. Bake for 1 hour and 45 minutes longer, brushing occasionally with orange juice mixture. Place the goose on a platter. Drain fat from roasting pan. Combine 2 tablespoons drippings, remaining orange juice and marmalade in a saucepan and heat through. Serve with goose. 8 servings.

Roast Goose with Pickle-Spiced Stuffing (above)

KIDNEY BEANS IN RED WINE

2 c. dried red kidney beans	**2 tbsp. butter**
4 slices bacon, diced	**2 tbsp. flour**
1 tsp. salt	**Pepper to taste**
1 tbsp. grated onion	**1 c. dry red wine**

Place the beans in a saucepan and cover with water. Soak overnight. Add enough water to cover. Add the bacon and salt and bring to a boil. Reduce heat and cover. Simmer for 2 hours. Drain and keep hot. Saute the onion in butter in a saucepan for 5 minutes. Add the flour and pepper and mix. Add the wine and cook until thickened, stirring constantly. Blend with beans. 6 servings.

Mrs. Ella S. Ballard, Clayton, New Mexico

PARMESAN BEANS WITH CROUTONS

3/4 c. bread cubes	**1/4 tsp. salt**
3 tbsp. salad oil	**1 No. 2 can cut green beans, drained**
1 tbsp. vinegar	**2 to 3 tbsp. grated Parmesan**
1 tsp. minced onion	**cheese**

Saute the bread cubes in 2 tablespoons oil in a saucepan until brown. Blend remaining oil with vinegar, onion and salt. Add the beans to bread cubes and cover with vinegar mixture. Heat through, stirring frequently, and place in a bowl. Sprinkle with cheese and serve.

Mrs. Jo Ann Gray, Waxahachie, Texas

BARBECUED CORN

8 ears of corn	**1 stick butter**
1/4 c. barbecue sauce	

Remove husks from the corn. Blend the barbecue sauce and butter and spread over each ear generously. Wrap each ear of corn securely in heavy-duty aluminum foil. Cook over hot coals for 15 to 20 minutes, turning several times.

Mrs. Jo-Ann T. Charping, Greenville, South Carolina

CORN SOUFFLE

1/4 c. butter	**3 eggs, separated**
1/4 c. flour	**1/2 tsp. salt**
2/3 c. milk	**1/4 c. grated cheese**
1 c. sieved cooked corn	**1 tbsp. chopped green pepper**

Melt the butter in a saucepan. Add the flour and stir until smooth. Add the milk and corn and cook until thick, stirring occasionally. Remove from heat and stir in beaten egg yolks, salt, cheese and green pepper. Fold in stiffly beaten egg whites and pour into a greased baking dish. Bake at 350 degrees for 30 minutes. Serve hot. 6 servings.

Dicia Blevins, Calhoun, Tennessee

Harvest Squash Ring (below); Cream of Pumpkin Soup (page 137);
Spicy Squash Pie (page 152)

HARVEST SQUASH RING

6 c. yellow squash	1 tbsp. Worcestershire sauce
1 med. onion, diced	1/2 tsp. pepper
1/2 med. green pepper, diced	1/2 tsp. hot sauce
1 clove of garlic, diced	1 c. bread crumbs
1 tsp. salt	3 eggs, well beaten
2 tbsp. sugar	1/2 c. milk
1/4 c. butter	

Cut the squash in 1/2-inch pieces and place in a saucepan. Add the onion, green pepper, garlic and enough boiling water to cover and cook until tender. Drain. Add remaining ingredients and mix well. Place in a greased 1 1/2-quart ring mold and place the mold in a pan of water. Bake at 350 degrees for 45 minutes. Unmold and fill center of ring with parsley. Garnish around ring with cooked green beans. 12 servings.

ACORN SQUASH STUFFED WITH HAM

3 med. acorn squash	2 c. diced cooked ham
1/2 tsp. salt	1 tsp. dry mustard
1 c. diced tart apples	1/4 tsp. pepper

Preheat oven to 425 degrees. Wash the squash and cut in halves lengthwise. Remove seeds and sprinkle squash cavities with salt. Place, cut side down, in a baking pan and add 1/4 inch boiling water. Bake for 30 minutes or until almost tender. Turn squash, cut side up. Combine remaining ingredients and spoon into squash cavities. Reduce temperature to 375 degrees and bake for 20 minutes longer or until apples are tender.

Mrs. Edith M. Davis, El Paso, Texas

Sweet Potato-Stuffed Apples (below)

SWEET POTATO-STUFFED APPLES

4 apples	Pinch of salt
1/4 c. red cinnamon candies	1/4 c. (packed) brown sugar
3/4 c. sugar	1/4 c. chopped pecans
1/2 c. water	4 lge. marshmallows
1 c. mashed sweet potatoes	

Core the apples and peel. Combine the candies, sugar and water in a saucepan large enough to hold apples. Cook over moderate heat for about 15 minutes or until candies are dissolved and syrup thickened. Place the apples in syrup and simmer until apples are partially cooked. Remove the apples from saucepan and place in a baking dish. Reserve syrup. Combine the sweet potatoes, salt, brown sugar and pecans. Stuff apples with potato mixture and pour reserved syrup over top. Bake at 350 degrees for 25 to 30 minutes or until apples are tender, basting frequently. Place a marshmallow on top of each apple and bake for 5 minutes longer or until marshmallows are brown.

NOVEMBER FIG BREAD

1 c. dried figs	3 tbsp. shortening
3 1/2 c. sifted all-purpose flour	1 tsp. grated orange rind
3/4 c. sugar	1 egg
1 tsp. salt	1 1/2 c. milk
4 tsp. baking powder	

Preheat oven to 375 degrees. Cover figs with boiling water and let stand for 10 minutes. Drain and dry thoroughly. Remove stems and cut figs in thin slices. Sift the flour with sugar, salt and baking powder into a bowl. Cut in the shortening until mixture resembles coarse cornmeal. Mix the orange rind with egg and milk.

Add to flour mixture and stir until just blended. Stir in figs and pour into a greased and brown paper-lined 9 x 5 x 3-inch loaf pan. Bake for 50 to 60 minutes or until golden brown.

Mrs. Orrin Thomas, Lake Charles, Louisiana

VERONA LOAF

3 3/4 to 4 1/4 c. unsifted flour	1/4 c. softened margarine
Sugar	3/4 c. hot water
1 tsp. salt	3 eggs, at room temperature
1 tbsp. grated lemon peel	1 1/2 tsp. vanilla
2 pkg. dry yeast	1/4 c. cold margarine

Mix 1 cup flour, 1/3 cup sugar, salt, lemon peel and yeast thoroughly in a large bowl. Add the softened margarine. Add the water gradually and beat with electric mixer at medium speed for 2 minutes, scraping bowl occasionally. Add the eggs, vanilla and 1/2 cup flour and beat at high speed for 2 minutes, scraping bowl occasionally. Stir in enough remaining flour to make a soft dough. Cover and let rise in a warm place, free from draft, for about 45 minutes or until doubled in bulk. Turn out onto a well-floured board and roll to a 1/2-inch thick rectangle. Cut 2 tablespoons cold margarine in small pieces and place on center 1/3 of the dough. Fold 1/3 of the dough over margarine. Cut remaining cold margarine in small pieces and place on top of folded third of dough. Bring remaining 1/3 of the dough over to cover margarine and roll dough out to an 18-inch strip. Fold into thirds and wrap loosely in waxed paper. Refrigerate for 20 minutes. Repeat rolling dough to an 18-inch long strip and folding into thirds twice. Place on a floured board and divide in half. Knead each half lightly and shape into a ball. Place each ball in a greased 8-inch round cake pan. Cover and let rise in a warm place, free from draft, for about 35 minutes or until doubled in bulk. Bake in a 350-degree oven for 35 to 40 minutes or until done. Remove from pans and sprinkle with sugar. Cool on wire racks.

Verona Loaf (above)

HORNS OF PLENTY

2 tbsp. cooking oil	2 eggs, slightly beaten
1/2 c. water	1 1/2 c. pancake flour
1 c. milk	

Mix first 4 ingredients in a bowl. Add the pancake flour gradually and beat until smooth. Pour onto hot griddle, making pancakes 6 inches in diameter, and cook until brown on both sides. Roll cornucopia-fashion as soon as cooked and fasten small end with toothpick. Fill with creamed ham, creamed tuna or creamed chicken. 6 servings.

Mrs. Oscar Chunn, Gadsden, Alabama

SPICY SQUASH PIE

1 c. (packed) brown sugar	1 1/2 c. canned squash
1 tbsp. flour	1 egg, beaten
1/2 tsp. salt	1 1/2 c. scalded milk
1/8 tsp. allspice	1 9-in. pie crust
1/8 tsp. each cloves and nutmeg	Pecan halves
1/8 tsp. each cinnamon and ginger	

Combine the brown sugar, flour, salt, spices and squash in a bowl and mix thoroughly. Add the egg and mix well. Stir in milk and pour into pie crust. Bake at 450 degrees for 30 to 40 minutes or until knife inserted in center comes out clean. Garnish with pecan halves.

Photograph for this recipe on page 149.

APPLE DUMPLINGS

2 2/3 c. sifted flour	1/3 c. chopped pecans
1 1/4 tsp. salt	1/4 tsp. nutmeg
1 c. shortening	6 med. tart apples
1/2 c. red cinnamon candies	Cream
Confectioners' sugar	

Mix the flour and salt in a bowl and cut in the shortening until mixture resembles coarse cornmeal. Sprinkle with 6 1/2 tablespoons cold water and mix well. Divide into 6 equal parts. Roll out each part on a floured surface to a 7-inch square. Place the cinnamon candies and 1/4 cup water in a saucepan and cook, stirring constantly, until candies are melted. Add 1/3 cup confectioners' sugar, pecans and nutmeg. Peel and core the apples. Place 1 apple on each pastry square and fill cavity with pecan mixture. Moisten edges of square with cream. Bring opposite corners of pastry over apple and press together. Repeat with remaining corners and brush dumplings with cream. Place on a baking sheet. Bake at 400 degrees for about 35 minutes or until brown. Mix 2 cups confectioners' sugar with enough cream to just moisten. Spoon onto hot dumplings and garnish dumplings with apple slices.

Photograph for this recipe on cover.

PUMPKIN-ORANGE CHIFFON PIE

1 c. sifted all-purpose
   flour
1/4 tsp. salt
3 tbsp. butter
2 tbsp. lard
Milk
1 c. sugar
1 tbsp. unflavored gelatin
1/2 tsp. ginger

1/2 tsp. cinnamon
1/2 tsp. nutmeg
3 eggs, separated
1 1/4 c. mashed cooked
   pumpkin
1 tsp. grated orange rind
1/4 c. orange juice
Sweetened whipped cream

Preheat oven to 450 degrees. Sift the flour and salt together into a mixing bowl. Cut in the butter and lard until mixture resembles small peas. Sprinkle 3 tablespoons milk over flour mixture, 1 tablespoon at a time, mixing lightly with fork after each addition. Shape into a ball. Flatten dough slightly on a lightly floured board, and roll out 1/8 inch thick in a circle 1 inch larger than a 9-inch pie plate. Place in the pie plate. Fold extra dough under and flute edge. Prick bottom and sides well with a fork. Bake for 10 minutes or until lightly browned, then cool. Mix 1/2 cup sugar, gelatin, ginger, cinnamon and nutmeg in a 2-quart saucepan. Beat the egg yolks in a bowl and stir in 1/2 cup milk. Add to gelatin mixture and cook over medium heat, stirring constantly, until mixture comes to a boil. Stir in the pumpkin, orange rind and orange juice and chill until partially set. Beat the egg whites until frothy. Add remaining sugar gradually and beat until stiff peaks form. Fold into pumpkin mixture and place in the pie crust. Chill for at least 6 hours or until firm. Serve with sweetened whipped cream and garnish with additional grated orange rind.

Pumpkin-Orange Chiffon Pie (above)

Candlelight Holiday Raisin Cake (page 179)

christmas

Christmas has always been more than just another holiday. It is a special atmosphere, an altered way of looking at the world, something so rare and unique it can only be called the "Christmas spirit." And in the Southland, the Christmas spirit prevails from just after Thanksgiving until "Old Christmas," January 5.

From Virginia — where the delightful holiday customs were kept alive during the two centuries when the rest of the nation did not celebrate Christmas — to the remote bayou regions of Louisiana — where people still adhere to the Gregorian calendar and hold that January 5 is Christmas — this season is a source of joyous pleasure for all.

Early in the holidays, fruit cakes are made from treasured recipes and packed into brightly decorated cake tins, tucked away in a cool, dark place, and left to ripen until the great holiday feast. Families plan in excited tones for the marvelous Christmas get-together, and everyone seeks that one perfect gift.

To help you capture the joyous spirit of a southern Christmas, *Southern Living* homemakers share their favorite holiday recipes with you in the section that follows. These are the recipes which have been handed down from one generation to another . . . the very finest southern Christmas recipes, now gathered for your family's pleasure.

Americans everywhere who take pleasure in their Christmas festivities owe an enormous debt to the Old South. For it was this region which kept alive the much-loved Christmas traditions when the rest of the nation abandoned them. In the beginning of our nation's history, there were two major areas of settlement. One, in New England, was dominated by Puritans, a hard-working and somber people who considered much of life's pleasures to be sinful. The other, in Virginia, was called a "cavalier" colony. Here people worked just as hard as their New England counterparts, but they accepted the joys of life as their reward for such hard work. In New England, there prevailed the Puritan tradition of considering Christmas just another day for hard work. Even such time-honored customs as the wassail bowl and the Yule log – ancient Christmas festivities in England – were abandoned as the

entertaining

FOR CHRISTMAS

industrious settlers went about their daily labors.

It remained for Virginia to preserve not only these holiday traditions but others equally well-loved. As time passed and settlers moved out of Virginia into the "West" – Tennessee and the Carolinas – and the Deep South, Christmas festivities were carried into these new settlements and were modified to fit the New World.

In England the wassail bowl had been a central feature of Christmas celebrations. It sat in the home on Christmas Eve, waiting to offer warm cheer to all who might enter. The innovative Virginians developed their own version of the wassail bowl – a rich brew known as eggnog. One old-time recipe called for equal parts of rye whiskey and Jamaica rum mixed with eggs and heavy cream and then amply laced with sherry! An echo of this tradition appears in the menu for Christmas Eve Supper on page 7 which begins with Cheery Wassail Bowl.

In many parts of America, Christmas Eve wouldn't be complete without the carolers who walk the streets singing ancient and much-loved Christmas songs. Caroling is another Christmas tradition which came out of the South. The French who settled in St. Louis and New Orleans brought the custom with them and shared it with their neighbors.

Firing arms was another southern holiday custom. In times past, the men of the neighborhood would gather early in the morning to hunt, shooting their muskets as they sought the local game. Today, firecrackers are set off instead of firearms. In villages and towns all over the South, this noise awakens families on Christmas morning. The holiday breakfast is still another Christ-

mas festivity. This, too, is a British custom preserved by the Virginians and now popular throughout the nation. The menu on page 7 features a typically southern holiday brunch with such foods as Southern-Fried Quail . . . Sausage with Apples . . . and Spiced Christmas Fruit.

After the excitement of a Christmas morning — complete with fireworks and the opening of presents — families throughout the Southland meet to enjoy Christmas Dinner. On page 7 you'll find a Christmas Dinner menu featuring foods certain to appear on southern tables from Maryland to Texas. Greengage Plum Salad . . . Roast Shoat with Hunter's Sauce . . . Rice Dressing and many other southern Christmas foods are featured.

While you're serving traditional foods, be sure to decorate your table in traditional fashion as well. Of course, you'll have the Christmas wreath on the door, but why not try one as a table centerpiece? Lay it flat and put great red candles in the center.

Red carnations and holly — which grows wild in southern woods — make an effective centerpiece when massed in a milkglass container. Or, for unusual elegance, feature an arrangement of white flowers in a silver bowl.

Small Christmas ornaments with names lettered in gold or silver nail polish make delightful take-home place cards. You might want to continue this Christmas ball decorating theme by filling a basket or bowl with ornaments and using it as a centerpiece.

Whatever you serve . . . however you decorate . . . your Christmas celebration owes a great deal to those southern families who kept holiday traditions alive during the first two hundred years of our country's settlement. From those families to yours, Merry Christmas.

Christmas Eve Punch (below)

∽ christmas eve ∽

CHRISTMAS EVE PUNCH

2 pt. fresh strawberries
4 eggs, separated
5/8 c. sugar
2 c. half and half
1 c. milk

3/4 c. orange juice
1/2 tsp. grated orange peel
Red food coloring
1 c. heavy cream, whipped

Puree the strawberries in electric blender at high speed and strain through a fine sieve to remove seeds. Beat the egg yolks and 1/2 cup sugar in a large mixing bowl until light and fluffy. Blend in the half and half, milk, orange juice, orange peel and pureed strawberries and add enough food coloring for desired tint. Beat the egg whites until soft peaks form. Add remaining sugar gradually and beat until stiff peaks form. Reserve several tablespoons meringue and whipped cream. Blend remaining meringue and whipped cream into the strawberry mixture and pour into a 4-quart punch bowl. Spoon reserved meringue and whipped cream on top and swirl gently with a flat knife or spatula. 24 cups.

CHEERY WASSAIL BOWL

2 c. sugar
4 c. water
12 whole cloves
4 sticks cinnamon
4 whole allspice

2 tbsp. chopped ginger
3 c. orange juice
2 c. lemon juice
2 qt. apple juice

Combine the sugar and water in a saucepan and boil for 10 minutes or until syrupy. Add the cloves, cinnamon, allspice and ginger and cover. Let stand in warm place for 1 hour. Add fruit juices and bring to boiling point. Strain and serve immediately.

Margaret Arnold, Gaithersburg, Maryland

SUPERB HOLIDAY EGGNOG

6 eggs, separated	Brandy flavoring to taste
1 pt. whipping cream	3/4 c. sugar
1 qt. milk	Nutmeg

Beat the egg whites in a large mixing bowl until soft peaks form. Beat the whipping cream in a small mixing bowl until stiff. Beat the egg yolks in another large mixing bowl until thick. Stir in the milk, flavoring and sugar. Fold in egg whites and whipped cream and pour into a punch bowl. Sprinkle generously with nutmeg. Brandy flavoring may be omitted and desired flavoring added. 12 servings.

Mrs. O. A. Covington, Paducah, Kentucky

FAR EAST SPICED TEA

1 gal. boiling water	1 sm. can frozen orange
2 sticks cinnamon	juice
3 cloves	1 sm. can frozen lemon
3 sm. tea bags	juice
1 1/2 to 2 c. sugar	

Combine the water, cinnamon, cloves and tea bags in a kettle and boil for 2 minutes. Remove from heat. Add the sugar and stir until dissolved. Strain. Add fruit juices and bring to a boil, stirring occasionally. Serve.

Lucille Sherard, Hartselle, Alabama

CRAB MEAT CANAPES

1 c. flaked crab meat	2 tbsp. minced parsley
2 tbsp. olive or corn oil	1/4 tsp. lemon juice
1 tsp. grated onion	3 or 4 green peppers

Place all ingredients except the green peppers in a blender and blend to a paste. Cut the green peppers in 1-inch squares and spread the crab meat mixture on green pepper squares. 4-6 servings.

Mrs. Roy Walters, Cape Coral, Florida

RED CAVIAR FORTE

1 4-oz. jar red caviar	3 tbsp. mayonnaise
1 med. onion, finely chopped	Juice of 1 lemon

Mix all ingredients in a bowl and chill. Serve with assorted crackers. 6 servings.

Mrs. Helen Foster, Lafayette, Louisiana

Ripe Olives for Little Parties (below)

RIPE OLIVES FOR LITTLE PARTIES

2 c. canned pitted ripe
   olives
2 8-oz. packages cream
   cheese
1 tsp. salt
6 drops of hot sauce
2 tbsp. lemon juice
2 tbsp. tomato paste
1/2 c. mashed avocado

8 candied cherries, chopped
1 tbsp. chopped sugared ginger
1/4 c. chopped nuts
1 bunch hearts of celery
1 cucumber
1 green pepper
1 tomato
1 red onion
1 pkg. Cheddar cheese

Chop 1 1/2 cups ripe olives very fine. Cut remaining olives into halves, quarters and rings for garnish. Soften the cream cheese in a bowl. Add the chopped olives, salt, hot sauce and lemon juice and mix well. Spoon equal amounts into 3 bowls. Add tomato paste to 1 bowl, mashed avocado to 1 bowl and cherries, ginger and nuts to remaining bowl. Stuff celery with cherry mixture and press together to form bunch. Roll in waxed paper and chill. Cut the cucumber into slices. Cut green pepper and tomato into wedges, scooping out seeds and membrane. Cut the onion into wedges and separate. Cut cheese into triangles. Pipe cream cheese mixtures onto canape bases with a pastry tube and garnish with reserved ripe olives. Cut celery into slices. Chill all canapes well before serving.

SHRIMP CHRISTMAS TREE

3 lb. shrimp
2 qt. boiling water
1/2 c. salt
4 lge. bunches curly endive
1 2 1/2-ft. high styrofoam cone

1 12 x 12 x 1-in. styrofoam
   square
1 sm. box round toothpicks
Cocktail sauce

Place the shrimp in boiling water and add the salt. Cover and simmer for about 5 minutes or until shrimp are pink and tender. Drain and cool. Peel the shrimp, leaving last section of shell. Remove sand veins and wash. Drain and chill. Separate the endive and wash. Drain and chill. Place the styrofoam cone in center of styrofoam square and draw a circle around base of cone. Cut out circle and insert cone in square. Cover base and cone with overlapping leaves of endive to resemble Christmas tree, starting at the outside edge of base and working up, and fasten endive to styrofoam with toothpick halves. Attach shrimp to tree with toothpicks. Serve cocktail sauce in a bowl for dunking.

SHRIMP AND OYSTER BISQUE

1 pt. oysters	1/2 tsp. minced parsley
2 c. finely chopped shrimp	Pinch of mace
5 c. milk	Salt and pepper to taste
1/2 c. chopped celery	3 tbsp. butter
3 tbsp. minced onion	3 tbsp. flour

Drain the oysters and reserve liquor. Chop the oysters fine and place in top of double boiler. Add the shrimp, reserved liquor, milk, celery, onion, parsley, mace, salt and pepper. Place over boiling water and cook for 30 minutes. Strain through a fine sieve. Melt the butter in a saucepan and stir in the flour. Stir in the strained oyster mixture and cook until thickened, stirring constantly. Do not boil. Serve in soup plates. Garnish each serving with 1 whole shrimp and dash of paprika, if desired.

Mrs. Betsy Dunn, Clarksdale, Mississippi

MAGI RICE SOUP

2 c. chopped onions	1/2 c. rice
1/2 lb. ground lamb	1 tsp. salt
3 tbsp. butter or margarine	1/2 tsp. paprika
1 qt. tomato juice	1 bay leaf
2 bouillon cubes	1/8 tsp. pepper

Saute the onions and lamb in butter in a saucepan until tender. Add remaining ingredients and bring to a boil, stirring occasionally. Reduce heat and simmer for 20 minutes.

Mrs. A. P. Idom, Morton, Mississippi

OYSTERS WITH CAVIAR

36 oysters	Minced green onion to taste
6 tbsp. black caviar	Lemon juice

Place 6 oysters on crushed ice on a plate for each serving. Spread 1/2 teaspoon caviar on each oyster and sprinkle with onion and lemon juice. 6 servings.

Mrs. B. N. Clinton, Little Rock, Arkansas

RAPHAEL SALAD

4 sm. cucumbers	8 red radishes, sliced
1/4 c. mayonnaise	1/2 c. olive oil
1/2 tsp. paprika	1 tsp. vinegar or lemon
1 med. head lettuce,	juice
shredded	1/4 tsp. salt
4 sm. tomatoes, quartered	Dash of garlic salt (opt.)
1 can asparagus tips, drained	

Peel and slice the cucumbers. Soak in cold, salted water for 30 minutes, then drain. Combine the mayonnaise and paprika and mix with lettuce. Line a salad bowl with lettuce mixture and cover with tomatoes, asparagus tips, radishes and cucumbers. Mix remaining ingredients and pour over salad. Cover with foil and refrigerate for 1 hour. 4 servings.

Mrs. Alta Forbess, Pineville, North Carolina

MIDNIGHT HOUR FRUIT SALAD

2 egg yolks	2 c. Royal Anne cherries
1/4 c. sugar	1 c. blanced slivered
1/4 c. cream	almonds
Juice of 2 lemons	1/2 lb. marshmallows,
1/8 tsp. salt	quartered
6 slices canned pineapple	1 c. heavy cream, whipped

Combine the egg yolks, sugar, cream, lemon juice and salt in top of a double boiler and place over boiling water. Cook, stirring constantly, until thick. Remove from heat and chill. Dice the pineapple and add to chilled mixture. Stir in remaining ingredients and refrigerate for 24 hours. Serve on lettuce leaves with mayonnaise, if desired. 12-14 servings.

Mrs. C. M. Brennan, Montgomery, Alabama

KOFTAS

1 med. onion, minced	1/4 tsp. ground cloves
1 med. sweet red pepper,	1/4 tsp. ground cardamom
minced	1/2 tsp. chili powder
1 clove of garlic, minced	1/2 tsp. hot sauce
2 tbsp. ground coriander	1 lb. ground chuck
2 tsp. salt	4 tbsp. butter or margarine
1/2 tsp. cinnamon	

Combine the onion, red pepper, garlic, coriander, salt, cinnamon, cloves, cardamom, chili powder and hot sauce and mix well. Add the ground chuck and mix thoroughly. Shape into 1-inch balls. Melt the butter in a skillet. Add the meatballs and brown over high heat, turning frequently. 4 servings.

Mrs. M. J. Blount, Mobile, Alabama

Swedish Meatballs (below)

SWEDISH MEATBALLS

1 lb. ground chuck	1 2/3 c. evaporated milk
1/4 c. fine dry bread crumbs	3 tbsp. butter
1 tbsp. instant minced onion	2 tbsp. flour
1 tsp. salt	1 beef bouillon cube
Dash of pepper	1 c. boiling water
1/2 tsp. allspice	1 tbsp. Worcestershire sauce

Mix the ground chuck, bread crumbs, onion, salt, pepper, allspice and 2/3 cup milk and shape into meatballs, using 1 teaspoon meat mixture for each. Melt the butter in a large, heavy skillet over medium heat. Add the meatballs and cook, turning frequently, until brown on all sides. Remove skillet from heat. Sprinkle the flour over meatballs and stir to blend well. Dissolve the bouillon cube in boiling water and add to skillet. Stir in remaining milk and the Worcestershire sauce and cook over low heat, stirring frequently, until thickened. Serve over hot, cooked noodles. 6 servings.

VEAL BALLS WITH SOUR CREAM

1 lb. ground veal	1/2 c. round buttery cracker
1 clove of garlic, minced	crumbs
2 tsp. chopped parsley	1/4 c. butter
1 tsp. salt	1/2 lb. mushrooms
1/4 c. milk	1 pt. sour cream

Combine the veal, garlic, parsley, salt, milk and cracker crumbs and shape into balls. Melt the butter in a skillet and brown meatballs and mushrooms in butter. Place in a casserole and add the sour cream. Cover. Bake in 350-degree oven for 1 hour. Serve with noodles and garnish with almonds. 6 servings.

Mrs. Douglas E. Pope, Louisville, Kentucky

163

VEAL CUTLETS IN SHERRY

2 lb. thin veal cutlets	**1/4 c. olive oil**
Salt, pepper and paprika	**1 clove of garlic, mashed**
to taste	**1 c. dry sherry**
1 1/2 c. grated Parmesan	**2 c. cooked peas**
cheese	

Pound the veal cutlets very thin with flat side of cleaver and cut in individual servings. Sprinkle with salt, pepper, paprika and Parmesan cheese and pound gently with a wooden mallet. Heat olive oil and garlic in a large skillet. Add the cutlets and brown over high heat. Cover with sherry and bring to a boil. Remove cutlets to a hot platter and pour sauce over cutlets. Cover with peas and sprinkle with additional Parmesan cheese. 6 servings.

Mrs. Donald M. Teer, Refugio, Texas

CORNED BEEF CASSEROLE

1 1-lb. can cut green	**1/2 tsp. crumbled savory**
beans	**2 c. diced cooked corned**
1/3 c. butter or margarine	**beef**
1/3 c. flour	**1 c. sliced cooked carrots**
1 1/2 c. milk	**4 c. hot mashed potatoes**
1/2 c. beef broth	**1 tsp. onion powder**
1 tbsp. prepared horseradish	**1 egg yolk, beaten**

Drain the beans, reserving 1/2 cup liquid. Melt the butter in a saucepan and blend in the flour until smooth. Stir in reserved bean liquid, milk and beef broth and cook, stirring, until thickened. Stir in the horseradish and savory. Fold in the beans, corned beef and carrots and turn into a 2 1/2-quart shallow casserole. Blend the potatoes with onion powder and egg yolk and pipe or spoon over casserole. Bake at 425 degrees for 20 minutes or until lightly browned and bubbling hot. Yield: 6 servings.

Mrs. Willie Smith, Fort Worth, Texas

CITRUS-HONEY PEAS

1 1/2 tsp. grated orange	**Juice of 1 lemon**
rind	**1/4 c. honey**
1 1/2 tsp. grated lemon	**1 No. 303 can green peas,**
rind	**drained**
2 tbsp. butter	**1/4 c. chopped pimento**
Juice of 1 orange	

Saute the grated rinds in butter in a saucepan for 2 to 3 minutes, then stir in fruit juices and honey. Cook over high heat for several minutes or until thickened. Add the peas and pimento and heat through. 4 servings.

Mrs. Marie Hayes, Atlanta, Georgia

CREAMED ONIONS WITH MUSHROOMS

2 tbsp. butter	2 tbsp. chopped parsley
2 tbsp. flour	10 med. cooked onions
1 c. milk	1/2 c. sliced mushrooms
1/4 tsp. salt	1/2 tsp. lemon juice
1/8 tsp. paprika	1/2 tsp. grated lemon rind

Melt the butter in a saucepan and stir in the flour. Add the milk and cook until thickened, stirring constantly. Add the salt, paprika and parsley. Combine the onions, mushrooms, lemon juice and rind in a bowl and pour the white sauce over onion mixture.

Mrs. Anna Benda Whitescarver, Flemington, West Virginia

POPPY SEED BRAIDED BREAD

1 pkg. yeast	3/4 c. warm milk
1/4 c. lukewarm water	1 well-beaten egg
1/4 c. soft butter or	3 1/2 c. flour
margarine	Melted butter or margarine
3 tbsp. sugar	Poppy seed
2 tsp. salt	

Dissolve the yeast in lukewarm water. Mix the butter, sugar, salt, milk and egg in a large mixing bowl and stir in the yeast. Add the flour and mix well. Cover and let rise for 10 minutes. Knead on a floured surface for 5 to 7 minutes. Place in the mixing bowl and let rise until doubled in bulk. Divide into 2 parts and roll out into rectangles. Brush well with melted butter and sprinkle with poppy seed. Cut each rectangle into 3 strips and braid. Place on a baking sheet and let rise for 30 to 40 minutes. Bake in 400-degree oven for 20 to 25 minutes. 2 loaves.

Photograph for this recipe on page 99.

FLAMING MINIATURE CREAM PUFFS

1 c. boiling water	4 eggs
1/2 c. shortening	2 qt. ice cream
1/2 tsp. salt	Raspberry sauce
1 c. sifted flour	1/4 c. curacao (opt.)

Preheat oven to 375 degrees. Combine the water, shortening and salt in a saucepan and bring to a boil. Add the flour all at once and stir vigorously over low heat for 1 minute or until mixture leaves side of pan. Remove from heat and beat for about 2 minutes. Add the eggs, one a a time, beating well after each addition, and beat until satiny. Drop from tablespoon onto an ungreased baking sheet 2 inches apart, making 16 mounds and swirling each as dropped from spoon. Bake for 50 minutes or until browned and puffy. Make a small slit in each puff with a knife and cool on cake rack. Split cream puffs through the side and fill each cream puff with ice cream. Place in freezer until ready to serve. Remove from freezer and place pyramid-fashion on a serving platter. Pour raspberry sauce over pyramid. Warm the curacao in a small saucepan and ignite. Pour over raspberry sauce.

Mrs. James Myers, Leesville, Louisiana

Raisin Pots de Creme au Chocolate (below)

RAISIN POTS DE CREME AU CHOCOLATE

2/3 c. dark seedless raisins
4   1-oz. squares semisweet
    chocolate

4 eggs, separated
Whipped cream

Chop the raisins coarsely. Melt the chocolate. Beat the egg yolks into melted chocolate, one at a time, then stir in the raisins. Beat the egg whites until stiff and fold into raisin mixture until well mixed. Spoon into souffle dishes and chill until firm. Garnish with whipped cream. 4 servings.

∽ christmas brunch ∾

SPICED CHRISTMAS FRUIT

1   1-lb. can whole apricots
1   1-lb. can pear halves
1   1-lb. can greengage
    plums
1   1-lb. can peach halves
1   1-lb. can sliced
    pineapple
1 tsp. aniseed

2 cinnamon sticks
3 tbsp. lemon juice
1/3 c. grenadine
1   8 3/4-oz. can black
    sweet cherries, drained
1   8 3/4-oz. can grapes,
    drained
1 lime, sliced

Drain first 5 ingredients and reserve syrups. Add aniseed and cinnamon sticks to reserved syrups in a saucepan and bring to a boil. Simmer for 10 minutes, then strain, reserving cinnamon. Add lemon juice and grenadine to syrup. Cut pine-apple slices in half and place in a bowl. Add the apricots, pears, plums, peaches, cherries and grapes and pour syrup over top. Add reserved cinnamon sticks and lime slices. Chill for several hours. 12 servings.

Mrs. Bill Jack Evans, Bowie, Texas

RED VELVET COCKTAIL

4 c. tomato juice	2 tbsp. lemon juice
1/2 c. minced onion	2 tbsp. Worcestershire sauce
1/2 c. chopped celery	1 tsp. hot sauce

Mix all ingredients and refrigerate for several hours. Strain and serve. 8-10 servings.

Mrs. Dorothy Shelton, Atlanta, Louisiana

CHRISTMAS MORNING PINEAPPLE QUICHE

1 10-oz. package pastry mix	1/8 tsp. white pepper
1 13 1/4-oz. can crushed	4 drops of hot sauce
pineapple	2 c. grated Swiss processed
3 eggs, lightly beaten	cheese
1 3/4 c. half and half	6 slices crisp bacon,
1 1/4 tsp. salt	crumbled

Preheat oven to 425 degrees. Prepare pastry mix according to package directions and divide into 4 portions. Roll out each portion on a floured surface to a 7 1/2-inch circle and fit into four 6-inch quiche pans. Drain the pineapple thoroughly, pressing out excess syrup. Combine the eggs with half and half, salt, pepper, hot sauce, pineapple and cheese. Turn into pastry-lined pans and top with bacon. Bake for about 25 minutes or until set in center. 4 servings.

Christmas Morning Pineapple Quiche (above)

SAUSAGE WITH APPLES

2 lb. smoked sausage links	Sugar to taste
3 cans sliced pie apples	Cinnamon to taste

Cut the sausage in 2-inch lengths and place in a cold electric skillet. Set temperature control at 300 degrees and cook for 5 minutes or until sausage is brown, turning frequently. Remove sausage from skillet and drain off all except 2 tablespoons drippings from skillet. Drain the apples. Add the sugar and stir gently so that apples remain in rings. Cook the apples in drippings in the skillet until brown, then place in a chafing dish. Add the sausage and sprinkle with cinnamon.

Mrs. M. F. Hammond, West Palm Beach, Florida

SOUTHERN-FRIED QUAIL

Quail	Flour
Salt and pepper to taste	

Season the quail with salt and pepper and dredge with flour. Cook in large frying pan in 1 inch of fat over high heat for several minutes. Cover and reduce heat. Cook, turning frequently, until golden brown. Drain on absorbent paper. Serve on a hot platter and garnish with lemon slices and parsley sprigs.

Mrs. Mae B. Plemmons, Chester, South Carolina

EGGS WITH GOLDEN MUSHROOMS

1 doz. eggs	2 tbsp. butter
1/4 c. cream	2 lge. cans broiled mushrooms,
Pinch of rosemary	drained
Salt and pepper to taste	

Combine the eggs, cream, rosemary, salt and pepper in a bowl and beat with a rotary beater until fluffy. Heat the butter in a skillet. Add the egg mixture and cook over low heat, stirring constantly, until eggs are soft scrambled. Stir in the mushrooms and serve immediately.

Mrs. C. Burke Herbert, Greenville, Alabama

HOT HOLIDAY DEVILED EGGS

20 hard-cooked eggs	1 1/2 tbsp. vinegar
1 tbsp. prepared mustard	Salt and pepper to taste
1/4 tsp. pepper	Pimento strips
1/4 c. mayonnaise	1/2 to 1 c. broth

Cut the eggs in half lengthwise. Remove yolks and sieve. Place in a bowl. Add the mustard, pepper, mayonnaise and vinegar and beat until smooth. Add the salt and pepper and mix. Fill the egg whites and garnish with pimento. Place in a chafing dish and add just enough broth to cover bottom of dish. Cover and heat for 15 minutes. 40 servings.

Mrs. Delores McEnearey, Maxwell AFB, Alabama

CRISP HOLIDAY WAFFLES

1 c. pancake mix	1 egg
2 tbsp. oil or melted	1 1/4 c. milk
shortening	Currant jelly

Place the pancake mix in a bowl. Add the shortening, egg and milk and stir until smooth. Bake in hot waffle iron for 10 minutes and serve with currant jelly.

Clara Thompson, Abbeville, Mississippi

STEAMED FIG PUDDING

1/3 c. shortening	1/2 c. chopped nuts
2/3 c. sugar	1/2 tsp. salt
2 eggs, beaten	2 tsp. baking powder
1 c. chopped dried figs	4 c. graham cracker crumbs
1/3 c. diced candied orange	1 c. milk
peel	1 recipe hard sauce
1/4 c. finely chopped citron	

Cream the shortening and sugar in a bowl. Add the eggs and mix well. Stir in the figs, orange peel, citron and nuts. Combine the salt, baking powder and cracker crumbs and add to creamed mixture alternately with milk. Place in a greased 6-cup mold and cover. Steam for 3 hours. Unmold and serve with hard sauce. 10-12 servings.

Steamed Fig Pudding (above)

ALMOND-FILLED CREPES

1/3 c. sifted flour	1 egg yolk
1 tbsp. sugar	3/4 c. milk
Dash of salt	1 tbsp. melted margarine
1 egg	

Place all ingredients in a mixing bowl and beat with an electric mixer until smooth. Refrigerate for several hours or until thick. Heat a heavy 6-inch skillet until a drop of water will dance on the surface. Grease lightly and pour in 2 tablespoons batter. Tilt skillet from side to side until batter covers the bottom. Cook for 1 minute and 30 seconds or until lightly browned. Invert skillet over paper towels. Cook remaining crepes in same manner.

Almond Filling

1 c. sugar	2 tsp. vanilla
1/4 c. flour	1/2 tsp. almond extract
1 c. milk	1/2 c. ground toasted almonds
2 eggs	Melted butter
2 egg yolks	Whipped cream
3 tbsp. margarine	

Mix the sugar and flour in a saucepan. Add milk and cook, stirring, until thick. Cook, stirring, for 2 minutes longer. Beat the eggs and egg yolks slightly. Stir small amount of hot mixture into the eggs, then stir back into the hot mixture. Bring to a boil, stirring, then remove from heat. Stir in remaining ingredients except melted butter and whipped cream and cool. Spread about 2 tablespoons almond mixture on unbrowned side of each crepe. Roll up and place, folded side down, in greased 13 x 9 x 2-inch baking dish. Brush with melted butter. Bake at 350 degrees for 20 to 25 minutes or until hot. Garnish with grated unsweetened chocolate and sifted confectioners' sugar. Serve warm with whipped cream. 10 crepes.

Mrs. Cary Stevens, Knoxville, Tennessee

ELVES' BLUEBERRY MUFFINS

2 2/3 c. flour	1 egg
1 c. blueberries	1/2 tsp. salt
1/4 c. butter	4 tsp. baking powder
1/4 c. sugar	1 c. milk

Mix 2/3 cup flour with blueberries and let stand for 1 hour. Cream the butter, sugar and egg in a bowl. Sift remaining flour with salt and baking powder and add to creamed mixture alternately with milk. Add floured blueberries and mix well. Place in greased muffin pans. Bake at 400 degrees for 25 minutes.

Gertrude Nichols, Eureka, Arkansas

∽ christmas day ∾

JULE-NISSE PUNCH

1 c. sugar
1 c. water
4 c. cranberry juice
1 1/2 c. lemon juice

2 c. orange juice
2 c. pineapple juice
1 qt. ginger ale

Combine the sugar and water in a saucepan and heat, stirring, until sugar is dissolved. Bring to a boil and reduce heat. Cover and cook for 5 minutes without stirring. Add fruit juices and chill thoroughly. Place ice in a punch bowl and pour in juice mixture. Stir in the ginger ale. 20 servings.

Mrs. Karen Moss, San Angelo, Texas

NOEL ESPRESSO CAFE

1 c. dark-roast pulverized
    coffee

2 c. water
Mint flavored whipped cream

Prepare the coffee in a drip coffee pot or an espresso pot, if available, using coffee and water. Add a dollop of cream to each cup of coffee. May be served with cream and sugar, if desired. 6 small cups.

Mrs. F. C. Adams, Beaufort, South Carolina

CELERIAC CONSOMME

6 c. chicken consomme
Cooked celery root, sliced thin

Finely chopped parsley

Bring consomme to a boil in a saucepan. Serve in heated soup plates and top with slices of celery root. Sprinkle each serving with 1 teaspoon parsley.

Mrs. Elton Mays, Bowie, Maryland

CHICKEN-HERB CONSOMME

3 tbsp. finely chopped
    chervil
3 tbsp. finely chopped
    parsley

2 tbsp. chopped chives
1 tbsp. chopped tarragon
4 c. hot chicken consomme
Thin lemon slices

Add chervil, parsley, chives and tarragon to the consomme in a saucepan and let steep for 2 minutes. Strain the soup and heat through. Serve with a slice of lemon in each cup.

Mrs. Howard Dark, Dover, Delaware

FROSTED GRAPES

Grapes	**Sugar**
1 egg white, slightly beaten	

Brush clusters of grapes with egg white and sprinkle with sugar. Let dry and arrange on a platter.

Mrs. William Chance, New Orleans, Louisiana

JERUSALEM ARTICHOKE PICKLES

1 gal. Jerusalem artichokes	**12 peppercorns**
1/4 c. salt	**Pickling spices**
4 cloves of garlic	**Vinegar**
8 red peppers	

Scrape the artichokes and cover with boiling water. Cool, then drain. Wipe artichokes dry. Place in a large container and cover with the salt. Place 1 clove of garlic, 2 red peppers, 3 peppercorns and desired amount of pickling spices in each of 4 sterilized quart jars and pack the artichokes into jars. Bring vinegar to a boil and pour into jars to cover artichokes. Seal at once.

Carman C. Buazeale, Natchitoches, Louisiana

HEAVENLY CHRISTMAS RELISH

1 gal. peeled ground pears	**2 pkg. powdered fruit pectin**
1 pkg. cranberries, ground	**14 c. sugar**
3 unpeeled oranges, ground	

Combine first 3 ingredients in a kettle and cook for 30 minutes. Add fruit pectin and sugar and cook for 10 minutes longer, stirring constantly. Place in sterilized jars and seal. 10 pints.

Mrs. Glen Hemphill, Ravenna, Texas

MARINATED CAULIFLOWER AND GREEN BEANS

1 10-oz. package frozen cauliflowerets	**1 hard-cooked egg, chopped**
1 9-oz. package frozen cut green beans	**1/3 c. cider vinegar**
2 tbsp. frozen chopped chives	**1/2 c. olive oil**
2 tbsp. frozen chopped parsley	**1 tsp. sugar**
	1 tsp. salt
	1/4 tsp. pepper

Cook the cauliflowerets and beans according to package directions and drain. Place in a glass bowl and add the chives, parsley and egg. Combine remaining ingredients and mix well. Pour over vegetable mixture and let stand at room temperature for at least 30 minutes, stirring occasionally. Serve immediately or refrigerate until ready to serve. 8 servings.

DILLED CARROTS

1 1-lb. package frozen whole baby carrots	1/3 c. lemon juice
2 tbsp. chopped fresh dill	1 tsp. sugar
1 clove of garlic, quartered	1 tsp. salt
1/3 c. olive oil	1/4 tsp. pepper

Cook the carrots according to package directions and drain. Place in a glass bowl and add the dill and garlic. Combine remaining ingredients and mix well. Pour over carrot mixture and toss lightly to coat evenly. Let stand at room temperature for at least 30 minutes, stirring occasionally. Remove garlic. Serve immediately or refrigerate until ready to serve. One-fourth cup dried dill sprigs may be substituted for fresh dill.

MUSHROOMS A LA GRECQUE

2 10-oz. packages frozen whole mushrooms, thawed	1/4 tsp. crumbled chervil
1/2 c. olive oil	1 bay leaf
1/2 c. cider vinegar	1 clove of garlic, quartered
1 tsp. salt	1 hard-cooked egg yolk, sieved
1/4 tsp. pepper	2 tbsp. drained capers

Place the mushrooms in a glass bowl. Combine remaining ingredients except egg yolk and capers in a saucepan and bring to a boil. Pour over mushrooms and let stand at room temperature for at least 30 minutes, stirring occasionally. Remove garlic and bay leaf and refrigerate until ready to serve. Stir in egg yolk and capers just before serving. 6 servings.

Marinated Cauliflower and Green Beans (page 172); Mushrooms a la Grecque (above); Dilled Carrots (above)

CRAB APPLE SALAD

1 3-oz. package cherry gelatin	1 1-lb. jar spiced crab apples
1 c. boiling water	1 tbsp. grated orange rind

Dissolve the gelatin in boiling water in a bowl. Drain the crab apples and reserve syrup. Add enough water to reserved syrup to make 3/4 cup liquid and stir into gelatin. Chill until partially set. Chop the apples and fold into gelatin. Fold in orange rind. Pour into individual molds and chill until firm. Serve with sour cream or mayonnaise. 12 servings.

Mrs. Marvin Boone, Bay Minette, Alabama

GREENGAGE PLUM SALAD

1 No. 2 1/2 can greengage plums	1/2 pt. whipping cream
1 pkg. lime gelatin	1/2 c. slivered blanched almonds
1 sm. package cream cheese	Lettuce

Drain the plums and reserve liquid. Add enough water to reserved liquid to make 2 cups liquid. Pour into a saucepan and bring to a boil. Remove from heat and stir in the gelatin until dissolved. Stir in the cream cheese until blended and chill until slightly thickened. Sieve the plums and stir pulp into gelatin. Fold in the whipped cream and almonds and place in a mold. Chill until firm and serve on lettuce.

Mrs. R. T. Martin, Nashville, Tennessee

ELEGANT OLIVE-CRAB MOUSSE

1 c. canned pitted ripe olives	2 tbsp. lemon juice
1 10-oz. package frozen asparagus spears	1/2 tsp. salt
	1/2 tsp. Worcestershire sauce
	Hot sauce to taste
2 env. unflavored gelatin	1/4 c. catsup
3/4 c. cold water	1 7 1/2-oz. can crab
1/2 c. mayonnaise	2 c. sour cream

Slice the olives. Cook the asparagus according to package directions until just tender and drain. Soften the gelatin in water in a saucepan. Place over low heat, stirring constantly, until gelatin is dissolved and remove from heat. Add to mayonnaise slowly, beating briskly, and blend in the lemon juice, salt, Worcestershire sauce, hot sauce and catsup. Drain and flake the crab. Reserve some ripe olive slices and asparagus spears for decoration. Cut remaining asparagus in small pieces and fold into gelatin mixture. Fold in remaining olives, sour cream and crab and chill until slightly thickened. Place reserved ripe olives in bottom of a 6-cup mold and cover with a small amount of thickened gelatin. Arrange reserved asparagus spears, tips down, against sides of mold and chill quickly. Spoon remaining gelatin mixture into mold and chill until firm. Unmold and garnish with salad greens and whole pitted ripe olives. 8-10 servings.

BROCCOLI WITH BRAZIL NUTS

1 pkg. frozen broccoli	1/2 tsp. salt
1/4 c. butter	Dash of hot sauce
1 tbsp. Worcestershire sauce	Toasted chopped Brazil nuts
2 tbsp. lemon juice	to taste

Cook the broccoli according to package directions and drain. Add remaining ingredients except nuts and heat through. Place in a serving bowl and sprinkle with Brazil nuts. Serve at once.

Mrs. Hannah Hoff Brown, Waco, Texas

RICE DRESSING

3/4 stick margarine	2 cans beef consomme
1 green pepper, chopped	Pepper to taste
1 onion, chopped	1 tsp. Italian seasoning
1/2 c. diced celery	1 4-oz. can mushrooms
1 c. rice	1 tsp. parsley
1/4 tsp. salt	1 can water chestnuts

Melt the margarine in a saucepan over low heat. Add the green pepper, onion and celery and cook for 10 minutes. Add remaining ingredients except water chestnuts. Drain the water chestnuts and slice. Stir into rice mixture and place in a casserole. Bake in 350-degree oven for 1 hour. 6 servings.

Mrs. R. B. Hays, Waynoka, Oklahoma

Elegant Olive-Crab Mousse (page 174)

Mushroom Stroganoff (below)

MUSHROOM STROGANOFF

2 lb. lean beef round or chuck	2 tsp. salt
1/2 c. butter	1/4 tsp. pepper
1 lb. fresh mushrooms, sliced	1 tbsp. Worcestershire sauce
1/2 c. diced mild onion	1 tbsp. cornstarch
1 6-oz. can tomato paste	2 tbsp. cold water
	1 c. sour cream

Cut the beef in 1/2-inch cubes and brown in butter in a large skillet over low heat. Add the mushrooms and onion and cook for 5 minutes. Add the tomato paste, salt, pepper and Worcestershire sauce and stir well. Cover and simmer for 1 hour or until beef is tender. Mix the cornstarch and water until smooth and stir into beef mixture. Cover and simmer for 10 minutes longer, stirring frequently. Blend the sour cream into beef mixture just before serving. 8 servings.

SOUR CREAM ROLLS

1 c. sour cream	1/2 c. sugar
1 1/2 pkg. yeast	1/2 tsp. salt
1/3 c. lukewarm water	4 c. flour
1 c. margarine, softened	2 eggs, well-beaten

Heat the sour cream in a double boiler until light yellow around edges. Dissolve the yeast in water. Mix the margarine, sugar and salt in a bowl. Pour the sour cream over margarine mixture and cool to lukewarm. Blend in 1 cup flour. Add the yeast and 1 cup flour and mix. Stir in eggs and remaining flour. Cover and refrigerate for 6 hours or overnight. Divide dough into 4 parts and roll each part into 1/4-inch thick circle. Cut each circle into 12 wedge-shaped pieces and roll each wedge from wide end toward point. Place on greased baking sheet, point side down, and curve into crescents. Let rise for 1 hour. Bake at 375 degrees for 15 minutes. 8-10 servings.

Mrs. Remmington McConnell, Atlanta, Georgia

GLAZED BAKED HAM

1 10 to 12-lb. fully cooked bone-in ham	1 whole gingerroot
	1 1/2 tsp. whole allspice
1 c. orange juice	Whole cloves
1 stick cinnamon	1/2 c. strained honey

Preheat oven to 325 degrees. Place the ham, fat side up, on a rack in a shallow roasting pan. Insert meat thermometer into center of thickest part of ham, being careful not to let thermometer touch the bone. Combine the orange juice, cinnamon, gingerroot, allspice and 1/2 teaspoon cloves in a small saucepan and bring to boiling point. Reduce heat and cover. Simmer for 5 minutes. Bake ham for 18 minutes per pound or to 130 degrees on meat thermometer, basting with spiced orange juice every 15 minutes. Score the fat of ham in 1-inch diamonds. Place a whole clove in center of each diamond and drizzle half the honey over the ham. Bake for 20 minutes. Drizzle remaining honey over ham and bake for 15 to 20 minutes longer or until golden brown. 20 servings.

Glazed Baked Ham (above)

ROAST SHOAT WITH HUNTER'S SAUCE

1 pig, 6 weeks old	1/2 tsp. thyme
Butter or margarine	1/2 tsp. sage
Pepper	3 tbsp. minced onion
2 c. toasted bread cubes	1/2 c. diced celery
1 c. mashed potatoes	Chicken broth

Have the butcher clean and dress the pig and reserve the liver. Scald the pig and rub dry. Rub with butter and pepper. Combine the bread cubes, potatoes, 1/8 teaspoon pepper, thyme and sage in a bowl. Cook the onion and celery in 1/4 cup butter in a saucepan until tender. Add to the bread mixture and toss until mixed. Add enough broth to moisten. Dice reserved liver and cook in small amount of butter until lightly browned. Stir into bread mixture and place in cavity of the pig. Sew up opening. Place pig in a roasting pan and add small amount of water. Hold body of pig in place with skewers. Roast at 325 degrees for about 4 hours or until tender. May place apple in pig's mouth just before serving.

Hunter's Sauce

1 c. red currant jelly	1/2 tsp. Worcestershire sauce
1/4 c. port	2 tbsp. butter or margarine
1/4 c. catsup	

Combine all ingredients in a small saucepan and heat until jelly and butter are melted and piping hot, stirring constantly. Serve warm with roasted pig.

Mrs. Joseph Dickerson, Raleigh, North Carolina

CHARLOTTE RUSSE

1 tbsp. unflavored gelatin	4 egg whites
1/4 c. cold water	3/4 c. sugar
1/4 c. boiling water	1 pt. heavy cream, whipped
Wine to taste	

Soften the gelatin in cold water. Add the boiling water and stir until dissolved. Add the wine and cool. Beat the egg whites until soft peaks form. Beat until stiff peaks form, adding 1/2 cup sugar gradually. Add remaining sugar to whipped cream gradually, then fold in egg whites. Fold in the gelatin and pour into a mold. Refrigerate for 2 hours or until firm. 8 servings.

Mrs. William W. Momyer, Randolph, Texas

TRADITIONAL AMBROSIA

12 oranges, sectioned	1 c. grated fresh coconut
1 No. 2 can crushed pineapple	

Place layers of orange sections and pineapple in a bowl, sprinkling each layer with coconut. Chill. 8 servings.

Mrs. Billie C. Carver, Woodsdale, North Carolina

CANDLELIGHT HOLIDAY RAISIN CAKE

1 1/4 c. shortening	1/2 tsp. ginger
1 1/4 c. honey	2 c. mixed diced candied fruits
6 eggs, well beaten	2 c. candied pineapple pieces
2 1/2 c. sifted flour	2 c. dark seedless raisins
1 tsp. salt	2 c. golden seedless raisins
1 tsp. baking powder	1 c. halved candied cherries
1 tsp. cinnamon	2 c. broken pecans
1/2 tsp. nutmeg	

Place the shortening and honey in a large bowl and beat until creamy and well blended. Stir in the eggs. Sift the flour with salt, baking powder and spices. Add to creamed mixture and stir until smooth. Blend in fruits and pecans and turn into a greased 10-inch tube pan lined with 2 thicknesses of greased heavy brown paper. Bake at 250 degrees for 4 hours to 4 hours and 30 minutes with shallow pan of water in bottom of oven. May be placed in three 8 1/2 x 4 1/2 x 2 1/2-inch loaf pans and baked at 300 degrees for about 2 hours.

Photograph for this recipe on page 154.

CHRISTMAS LANE CAKE

1/2 c. butter or margarine	3 c. flour
2 c. sugar	2 tsp. baking powder
1 tsp. vanilla	1/8 tsp. salt
1 tsp. almond flavoring	1 c. milk
7 egg whites	Filling

Cream the butter and sugar in a bowl and stir in vanilla and almond flavoring. Add the egg whites, one at a time, beating well after each addition. Sift dry ingredients together and add to creamed mixture alternately with milk. Pour into 4 waxed paper-lined, greased and floured 8-inch layer pans. Bake at 350 degrees for 25 to 30 minutes and cool. Spread Filling between layers and on top and side of cake.

Filling

1/2 lb. butter or margarine	1 c. shredded coconut
1 1/2 c. sugar	1 c. chopped English walnuts
7 egg yolks, well beaten	1 c. chopped pecans
1 c. raisins	1 tsp. vanilla

Melt the butter in top of a double boiler. Add the sugar and egg yolks and mix well. Cook over boiling water until thick, stirring constantly. Add raisins, coconut, walnuts, pecans and vanilla and mix.

Robbie Humphries, Vina, Alabama

Quick Choco-Mint Fudge (page 187)

gourmet christmas gifts

The very nicest gifts are those we prepare ourselves. Such gifts are a part of us . . . and through them we share our creativity with those we love. Southern homemakers know that nothing says "Merry Christmas" as well as gifts they have made in their kitchens. And here, in the pages that follow, are the recipes for gourmet holiday treats these women prepare with pride every Christmas season.

You'll discover delicious breads — what better gift than a fragrant loaf of homemade bread on its own cutting board. For a nice touch, attach the recipe so that the recipient can duplicate the gift in her own kitchen.

There are recipes for the sweets that are so much a part of holiday time: the shaped cookies decorated in eye-pleasing fashion, melt-in-the-mouth candies, and elegant cakes. Imagine the pride you'll feel in sharing the bounty of your cooking skill with others at Christmas.

Every recipe in this section is the pride and joy of the homemaker who now shares it with you. Some of these recipes have come down through many generations and are among the most cherished possessions of southern families. Others are as new as tomorrow, the product of a *Southern Living* homemaker's rich imagination. All are awaiting your cooking pleasure . . . and the pleased surprise of the people to whom they are given. Share a part of yourself this Christmas with gourmet Christmas gifts.

UNBAKED FRUITCAKE

1 1-lb. box graham crackers	1 c. chopped candied pineapple
3/4 c. milk	4 c. shelled Brazil nuts
1 lb. marshmallows	1 15-oz. box seedless raisins
1 c. chopped candied cherries	Sherry or cognac

Line 2 loaf pans with greased waxed paper. Crush the graham crackers fine with a rolling pin. Place the milk and marshmallows in a saucepan and place over low heat, stirring occasionally, until melted. Combine graham cracker crumbs, fruits, nuts and raisins in a large bowl. Pour marshmallow mixture over crumb mixture and mix thoroughly. Pack into prepared pans firmly and cover tops with waxed paper. Wrap in foil and store in refrigerator for 1 month, sprinkling with sherry about twice a week. Keeps in refrigerator for months or may be frozen.

Mrs. Carlos Cagle, Greensboro, North Carolina

ORANGE SLICE CAKE

1 c. butter	3 1/2 c. sifted flour
2 c. sugar	2 c. chopped nuts
2 tsp. grated orange rind	1 lb. candy orange slices, chopped
4 eggs	1/2 lb. chopped dates
1 tsp. soda	1 c. flaked coconut
1/2 c. buttermilk	

Cream the butter and sugar in a bowl and add the orange rind. Add the eggs, one at a time, beating well after each addition. Dissolve soda in buttermilk and add to creamed mixture alternately with flour. Add the nuts, orange slices, dates and coconut and mix well. Pour into a greased and floured tube pan. Bake at 300 degrees for 1 hour and 30 minutes or until done.

Glaze

1 c. orange juice	2 tsp. grated orange rind
2 c. powdered sugar	

Combine all ingredients and pour over hot cake. Cool cake in pan.

Mrs. Jim Dixon, Tampa, Florida

DATES PETIT PAIN

2 eggs, beaten	1/4 c. butter
1 c. sugar	2 c. oven-toasted rice cereal
Dash of salt	1 c. chopped nuts
1 lb. pitted dates, chopped	Shredded coconut

Mix the eggs and sugar in a saucepan. Add the salt, dates and butter and mix well. Cook over low heat for about 10 minutes, stirring constantly, and remove from heat. Add rice cereal and nuts and mix well. Drop by teaspoonfuls into coconut and roll. Form into shape of dates and cool.

Ramona Lawton, Savannah, Georgia

PINEAPPLE-STRAWBERRY JAM

1   12-oz. box frozen sliced
   strawberries, thawed
1 No. 2 can crushed pineapple
5 c. sugar
2 tbsp. lemon juice

1 tsp. grated lemon rind
1/2 bottle liquid fruit
   pectin
Melted paraffin

Combine the strawberries, pineapple, sugar, lemon juice and lemon rind in a saucepan. Bring to a boil and boil for 1 minute. Remove from heat and stir in fruit pectin. Stir and skim for 5 minutes. Ladle into sterilized jars and cover with paraffin. 9 glasses.

Mrs. Florence M. Klawitter, Atlanta, Georgia

NUIT NOEL CONSERVE

1 lge. orange
3 c. chopped pears
3/4 c. drained crushed
   pineapple
1/2 c. maraschino cherries
1/2 c. lemon juice

1/2 c. chopped nuts (opt.)
1 c. shredded coconut (opt.)
1 pkg. powdered fruit
   pectin
5 c. sugar

Remove seeds from orange and chop the orange. Place in a large saucepan. Add the pears, pineapple, cherries, lemon juice, nuts and coconut and stir in the pectin. Place over high heat and bring to a boil, stirring constantly. Add the sugar. Bring to a boil and boil for 1 minute, stirring constantly. Remove from heat and stir and skim for 5 minutes. Pour into hot, sterilized 1/2-pint jars and seal at once.

Sallie P. Satterly, Hitchins, Kentucky

PLUM MARMALADE

1 qt. plums, seeded
4 c. sugar
1 lb. ground raisins

2 oranges, ground
1/4 lb. chopped walnuts
Melted paraffin

Mix the plums, sugar, raisins and oranges in a saucepan and cook for 20 minutes. Cool. Add the walnuts and pour into sterilized jars. Cover with paraffin.

Marguerite Jackson, Anderson, South Carolina

Ginger Cookies (below), Swedish Sprintz (page 185)

GINGER COOKIES

2 1/2 c. sifted flour	1 1/2 tsp. ginger
1/2 tsp. soda	1/3 c. butter
1/2 tsp. salt	1/2 c. sugar
1/2 tsp. cinnamon	1/2 c. dark molasses
1/2 tsp. nutmeg	1 egg, beaten

Sift the flour, soda, salt and spices together. Cream the butter and sugar in a bowl until light and fluffy. Add the molasses and egg and blend well. Chill for several hours or overnight. Roll out on a lightly floured board or pastry cloth to 1/8-inch thickness and cut with a star-shaped cookie cutter. Place on a greased cookie sheet. Bake at 375 degrees for 10 to 12 minutes. 2 dozen.

FROSTY WINTER BARS

1 1/2 c. butter	1 c. graham cracker crumbs
1 c. sugar	Whole graham crackers
1 egg, well beaten	6 tbsp. light cream or
1/2 c. milk	evaporated milk
1 1/2 c. flaked coconut	1 tsp. vanilla
1 1/4 c. chopped pecans	2 c. powdered sugar

Melt 1 cup butter in a saucepan and stir in the sugar, egg and milk. Bring to a boil over low heat, stirring constantly, then remove from heat. Stir in the coconut, 1 cup pecans and graham cracker crumbs. Cover bottom of 13 x 9-inch baking dish with whole graham crackers and spread coconut mixture over crackers. Cover with whole graham crackers. Soften remaining butter in a bowl. Add the cream, vanilla and powdered sugar and beat until fluffy. Spread over crackers and sprinkle with remaining pecans. Refrigerate overnight and cut into bars. Cookies may be frozen.

Mrs. Thelma Maxey, Lorenzo, Texas

SWEDISH SPRINTZ

2 1/2 c. sifted flour	3/4 c. sugar
1/2 tsp. baking powder	1 egg
1/4 tsp. salt	1 tsp. vanilla
1 c. butter	

Sift the flour, baking powder and salt together. Cream the butter and sugar in a bowl until light and fluffy. Add the egg and vanilla and beat well. Add the flour mixture and blend well. Press through a cookie press onto a cold, ungreased cookie sheet. May be shaped into 3/4-inch balls and flattened on cookie sheet with a fork. Bake at 400 degrees for 5 to 8 minutes or until delicately browned. 4 1/2 dozen.

FRUITCAKE BONBONS

1 6-oz. can frozen orange juice concentrate, thawed	3 eggs
	1 1/4 c. sifted all-purpose flour
1/2 c. molasses	1/8 tsp. soda
1 15-oz. package raisins	1 tsp. cinnamon
1 1-lb. jar mixed candied fruits	1/2 tsp. nutmeg
	1/4 tsp. allspice
1/2 c. butter or margarine	1/4 tsp. ground cloves
2/3 c. sugar	1/2 c. chopped walnuts

Combine the orange juice concentrate, molasses and raisins in a saucepan and cook over medium heat, stirring occasionally, until mixture comes to a boil. Reduce heat and simmer for 5 minutes, stirring constantly. Remove from heat. Reserve 1/2 cup candied fruits for garnish. Stir remaining fruits into orange juice mixture. Cream the butter and sugar in a bowl, then beat in eggs, one at a time. Sift the flour, soda and spices together and stir into creamed mixture. Add the orange juice mixture and walnuts and mix well. Line 1 3/4-inch muffin cups with miniature paper liners. Place 1 tablespoon batter in each liner and top with 1 or 2 pieces of reserved fruits. Bake in 350-degree oven for 20 to 25 minutes. 7 1/2 dozen.

Mrs. Beverly Hodges, Albuquerque, New Mexico

DATE-FILLED CHEESE PASTRIES

1/2 c. butter	7 oz. pitted dates, chopped
1/4 lb. Cheddar cheese, grated	1/2 c. (packed) light brown sugar
1 c. flour	1/4 c. water

Cream the butter and cheese in a bowl and add the flour gradually. Shape into 2 long rolls and wrap in waxed paper. Chill overnight. Combine the dates, sugar, and water in saucepan and cook over low heat, stirring constantly, for about 5 minutes or until dates are soft. Cool, then chill. Slice chilled dough about 1/8 inch thick, several slices at a time, and spread half the slices with date filling. Place remaining slices on top and place on a baking sheet. Bake at 350 degrees for 15 to 18 minutes.

Flora Ward, Newville, Alabama

BABY SUGARPLUM BREAD

2 pkg. dry yeast	1/2 tsp. vanilla
1/3 c. warm water	1/4 tsp. nutmeg
1 c. scalded milk	1/2 c. chopped mixed
1/2 c. sugar	candied fruits
1/4 c. shortening	1 c. seedless raisins
1 1/2 tsp. salt	Confectioners' sugar icing
5 to 5 1/2 c. sifted flour	Walnut halves
2 eggs, beaten	

Dissolve the yeast in the water. Combine the milk, sugar, shortening and salt in a bowl and cool to lukewarm. Stir in 1 1/2 cups flour and beat vigorously. Add the eggs and beat well. Stir in the yeast, vanilla and nutmeg. Add the candied fruits, raisins, and enough remaining flour to make a soft dough. Place on a floured surface and knead for 6 to 8 minutes or until smooth and elastic. Place in a lightly greased bowl and turn once to grease the surface. Cover and let rise in a warm place for about 2 hours or until doubled in bulk. Punch down and divide in half. Cover and let rest for 10 minutes. Divide each half of the dough into 6 parts. Shape each part into 6 balls and place in greased muffin pans. Cover and let rise in a warm place for 45 to 60 minutes or until doubled in bulk. Bake at 350 degrees for about 20 minutes or until done. Drizzle the top of each with icing and garnish with a walnut half.

Francine Reynolds, Pine Bluff, Arkansas

PEAR RELISH

1 peck pears, chopped	1 tsp. turmeric
6 sweet red peppers, chopped	1 tsp. allspice
	1 qt. vinegar
6 med. onions, chopped	2 lb. sugar
3 stalks celery, chopped	1 tbsp. mustard seed
1 tbsp. salt	

Combine all ingredients in a kettle and bring to a boil. Reduce heat and cook over low heat for about 10 minutes, stirring frequently. Pour into sterilized jars and seal.

Mrs. Jennie Mae Grider, Gamaliel, Kentucky

PECAN BAISERS

1 egg white	1/2 tsp. vanilla
3/4 c. sugar or brown sugar	2 c. pecan or walnut halves

Beat the egg white in a bowl until soft peaks form. Beat in the brown sugar and vanilla gradually. Fold in the pecan halves and place on a greased cookie sheet. Bake in 250-degree oven for 30 minutes. Turn off heat and let set for 30 minutes. Break pecans apart and store in airtight container.

Mary E. Finley, Macclenny, Florida

CRANBERRY-ORANGE BREAD

3/4 c. sugar	3 c. prepared biscuit mix
1 egg	3/4 c. chopped nuts
1 1/4 c. orange juice	1 c. chopped fresh
1 tbsp. grated orange rind	cranberries

Preheat oven to 350 degrees. Mix the sugar, egg, orange juice, orange rind, and biscuit mix in a bowl and beat vigorously for 30 seconds. Mixture will be lumpy. Stir in the nuts and cranberries and pour into a well-greased 9 x 5 x 3-inch loaf pan. Bake for 55 to 60 minutes or until toothpick inserted in center comes out clean. Remove from pan and cool before slicing.

Mrs. Margaret Rose Barnett, Fort Knox, Kentucky

CHRISTMAS BREAD

2 c. flour	1 tbsp. grated orange
1 c. sugar	rind (opt.)
1 1/2 tsp. baking powder	1 egg, well beaten
1/2 tsp. soda	1/2 c. chopped nuts
1 tsp. salt	1 c. coarsely chopped
1/4 c. shortening	cranberries
3/4 c. orange juice	

Sift the flour, sugar, baking powder, soda and salt together into a bowl. Cut in shortening until mixture resembles coarse cornmeal. Combine the orange juice and orange rind with egg. Pour all at once into flour mixture and mix just enough to dampen dry ingredients. Fold in the nuts and cranberries and spoon into a greased 9 x 5 x 3-inch loaf pan. Spread corners and sides slightly higher than center. Bake at 350 degrees for 1 hour. Remove from pan and cool.

Mrs. Roy Blankenship, Nashville, Tennessee

QUICK CHOCO-MINT FUDGE

2 c. sugar	1 1/2 c. semisweet chocolate
3 tbsp. butter	pieces
1/2 tsp. salt	2/3 c. chopped pecans
1 c. evaporated milk	1/2 tsp. peppermint extract
1/2 c. miniature marshmallows	

Combine the sugar, butter, salt and milk in a large saucepan and bring to a boil over medium heat, stirring constantly. Boil, stirring, for 5 minutes and remove from heat. Add the marshmallows, chocolate, pecans and peppermint extract and stir until the marshmallows and chocolate are melted and blended. Pour into a greased 8-inch square pan and cool. Cut into squares. 2 pounds.

Photograph for this recipe on page 180.

Christmas Butter Fudge (below), Chocolate Fudge (below)

CHRISTMAS BUTTER FUDGE

4 c. sugar
2 c. milk
1/2 c. butter
1/4 tsp. salt
1 tsp. vanilla

1/4 c. finely chopped
   candied cherries
1/4 c. blanched pistachio
   nuts

Place the sugar, milk, butter and salt in a large saucepan and bring to boiling point, stirring constantly until sugar is dissolved. Cook over moderate heat, stirring occasionally, until mixture forms a soft ball when dropped into cold water or to 236 degrees on candy thermometer. Remove from heat and place pan in cold water. Do not stir or beat until cooled to lukewarm. Add the vanilla and beat until thick and creamy. Add the cherries and nuts and fold in quickly. Pour into a greased 8-inch square pan and let stand at room temperature until firm. Cut into squares and decorate with candied fruit, if desired. About 2 1/2 pounds.

CHOCOLATE FUDGE

1 1/4 c. milk
4   1-oz. squares unsweetened
   chocolate
3 c. sugar
2 tbsp. corn syrup

1/4 c. butter
1 tsp. vanilla
1 1/2 c. coarsely chopped
   nuts

Place the milk and chocolate in a heavy saucepan and place over low heat until chocolate is melted. Add the sugar and corn syrup and stir until sugar is dissolved. Wash sugar crystals from sides of pan with damp cloth wrapped around a fork. Cook to soft-ball stage or to 234 degrees on candy thermometer, stirring occasionally, and remove from heat. Add the butter and cool to lukewarm without stirring. Add the vanilla and nuts and stir until candy holds shape and begins to lose gloss. Pour into a greased platter or pan and cool until set. Cut into squares and decorate with pecan halves, if desired. About 3 pounds.

INDEX

PHOTOGRAPHY CREDITS: *U. S. Department of Commerce: National Marine Fisheries Service; Pet Milk Company; Campbell Soup Company; Standard Brands: Fleischmann's Yeast and Fleischmann's Margarine; Olive Administrative Committee; Pickle Packers International; Artichoke Advisory Board; National Cherry Growers and Industries Foundation; California Strawberry Advisory Board; South African Rock Lobster Service Corporation; California Avocado Advisory Board; United Fresh Fruit and Vegetable Association; Knox Gelatine; McIlhenny Company; Florida Citrus Commission; The Apple Pantry; California Raisin Advisory Board; Corning Glass Works; John Oster Manufacturing Company; Cling Peach Advisory Board; Diamond Walnut Kitchen; Brussels Sprouts Marketing Program; Spanish Green Olive Commission; Carnation Evaporated Milk; National Kraut Packers Association; National Macaroni Institute; Louisiana Yam Commission; Pineapple Growers Association; Standard Brands: Royal Puddings and Gelatins; National Association of Frozen Food Packers; Keith Thomas Company; Best Foods: A Division of Corn Products Company, International; Angostura-Wuppermann Corporation; Evaporated Milk Association; Sunkist Growers; California Beef Council; National Dairy Council; Ocean Spray Cranberries, Inc.; The Pillsbury Company; General Foods Kitchens; California Dried Fig Advisory Board; American Spice Trade Association.*